IN THE DEEP HEART'S CORE

In the

DEEP HEART'S CORE

MICHAEL JOHNSTON

With a Foreword by Robert Coles

GROVE PRESS
New York

Published simultaneously in Canada
Printed in the United States of America

FIRST EDITION

Library of Congress Cataloging-in-Publication Data
Johnston, Michael, 1974–
   In the deep heart's core / Michael Johnston ; with a foreword by Robert Coles.
—1st ed.
      p. cm.
   ISBN 0-8021-1721-X
   1. Johnston, Michael, 1974–   2. Greenville High School (Greenville, Miss.)
3. Teachers—Mississippi—Greenville—Biography.   4. Poor children—
Education (Secondary)—Mississippi—Greenville—Case studies.   I. Title.
LA2317.J625 A3 2002
373.11'009762'42—dc21   2002072246

Design by Laura Hammond Hough

Grove Press
841 Broadway
New York, NY 10003

02 03 04 05   10 9 8 7 6 5 4 3 2 1

FOR MOM AND DAD,

AND FOR THE STUDENTS OF GREENVILLE HIGH

I will arise and go now, for always night and day

I hear lake water lapping with low sounds by the shore;

While I stand on the roadway, or on the pavements grey,

I hear it in the deep heart's core.

—W. B. YEATS

If Mississippi is the heart of the Deep South,

then the Mississippi Delta is the deep heart's core.

—DELTA SAYING

Contents

Foreword

ROBERT COLES

Those who help boys and girls learn their letters and numbers are constantly learning themselves—to the point that a good teacher becomes a constantly avid student, eager to understand what is happening in the world of watching and listening to the young citizenry that is called a schoolroom. Yet not all teachers are ready and willing to summon their students in such a manner, to regard them as enablers of reflective awareness—hence the sem blance of military drill that is found in so much of elementary and high school education.

It is no wonder, then, that so many of us who have sent our children to school, or who have tried our best to work as teachers, will be especially grateful for this book of Michael Johnston's: his wonderfully accessible, candid account of what he learned as he tried to encourage others to learn, in a community so needy of the educational assistance he had to offer, yet at the same time so torn by its own long-standing divisions, doubts, and suspicions. In a sense, this is a book about the vocational hazards that often meet goodwill as it gets carried across barriers of race and class and geography in pursuit of a spell of living expression. As I first read the pages that follow, I kept recalling words spoken to some of us who went to Mississippi in 1964 in connection with the civil rights struggle by an African-American minister from Biloxi, where I once lived as an air force officer in 1958: "You come here as an outsider, and in no time you'll be caught in the middle of things. You'll get to know us here—and yourself, too."

Those words apply to all travelers, anxious to take note of what they find right before their eyes and within earshot. But that clergyman's tactful yet firmly stated comment (and warning) surely applies to the extraordinary witness that this book offers, that of an aspiring, conscientious educator who becomes all too abruptly a target of distancing doubt, if not outright derision. His generous intentions, his educational advantages willingly put on the line for others hungry for the teacher's food he had to tender daily, are regarded as virtually insurrectionary in nature. What Michael Johnston's "deep heart's core" was given to endure was the fulfillment of his teacherly work on the one hand—no matter the inevitable frustrations and disappointments that go with such classroom endeavors—and on the other, the isolation and even fearful scorn that was directed at him by casual strangers who he had every right to hope might be politely respectful fellow citizens, glad for his well-meant and earnestly proffered efforts.

As I was finishing this book, I remembered other words, those of the novelist Walker Percy, a one-time Greenville, Mississippi, resident whose second cousin, William Alexander Percy (the lawyer, gentleman farmer, poet, and essayist who wrote *Lanterns on the Levee: Recollections of a Planter's Son*), became an adoptive father for him: "I have fond memories of living in Greenville with Uncle Will, and hearing him talk about Mississippi—all the troubles, but the fine, fine folks there, too. He was always thinking of the children, all they needed, if they were going to grow up educated. It mattered to him that Greenville should have good schools, and a good public library. He would have loved to teach himself, but he was all tied up with his own responsibilities. 'If I had another life,' he once told us, 'I'd go and read some of the books I have in my home to Greenville's children: tell them who wrote what, and why, get them excited about a poem, a story.'"

I can only imagine how pleased Walker Percy and his beloved Uncle Will would be, were they alive today and could read of Michael Johnston's journey into the "deep heart's core" of today's Greenville. It is a journey of personal and ethical affirmation very much like the one rendered in Percy's novel *The Moviegoer,* an attempt to find meaning and purpose during those early decades of life before a well-trodden path of work and more work becomes all-encompassing, and the point of things therefore irretrievably lost. My hunch tells me that both Percys, gone from us now but somewhere in this universe, are applauding this thoughtful outsider who became an insider all too aware of what was happening, and decided to make a difference. His book will help the rest of us learn so very much as we meet him, and come to know of his modestly rendered but compelling and important moral witness to educational efforts today.

Part One

INTO THE DELTA

I came to Mississippi to discover a story too complex to comprehend from pictures and too human to gather from the pages of
books. I had tried, reading and watching and studying the history
of this place, but each of these left me without a real sense of her. I
couldn't be convinced that Mississippi was home to a pernicious
root dug deep in the soil of America, planted by those who swore
allegiance to division and intolerance and acrimony. Nor could I
comprehend the violence and the vitriol that had built her reputation as the bastion of all that was most sinister about the South. I
had come to find the figure from which these two disparate shadows were cast.

A century ago my voyage into Mississippi would have been
by riverboat, Greenville being the next port city south of Memphis,
and the last before Vicksburg and then New Orleans. Then I might
have been a carpetbagger, searching the ruins of the decimated
South for some kind soil where I could harvest an American dream
someone else had planted. Fifty years ago I would have come by
train, riding that massive artery of the great migration that pumped
Mississippians north to Chicago and hurried them home again with
stories of urban promise. Then I might have been a freedom rider,
searching to wage a peaceful war against a history of hate. But today

3

I enter Mississippi on a twelve-seater prop plane from Memphis to Greenville. I have come to be a teacher, but despite the healing hand of time, despite my insistence that—raised in Colorado—I come from the West and not the North, I am still a Yankee.

The story of the African-American was at the center of everything I knew of Mississippi and everything I hoped to know. Mississippi fascinated me precisely because it was home to so many of the celebrated monuments and tragic memorials of the American struggle for civil rights. Over the centuries blacks have shaped Mississippi like the mighty river that gives the state its name: crafting lakes and floodplains, banks and flatlands, bringing floods and fecundity—they have been the source of its triumph and its tribulation. Land and water, black and white, transformation and perseverance, these were the things that made Mississippi magical.

But my journey was not just my own, not a solitary adventure to an introspective place, but a project weighted disproportionately with outward purpose. I had come to teach, because at age twenty-two education was the one valuable skill I could bring to Mississippi that she could use. It was the well-intended gift I offered for the privilege of room and board and revelation. There the stories run together, of Mississippi and migration and service, of race and class and education, of rivers and land and journeyman, of history and hatred and hope.

ONE

Two white women stood side by side inside the Enterprise Rent-A-Car office, a ticket-booth-sized building in a dirt parking lot. They smiled and extended a warm welcome. The three of us were well along in the business of renting a car without any exchange of personal information, when one looked up from the form and asked politely, "Place of employment?"

"Greenville High School."

It was the first time I had given an answer to that question that did not include "student."

The woman working behind the desk suddenly turned to me and exclaimed, "Oh! You poor thing!"

"What are you going to teach?" the other one asked in obvious surprise.

"English."

This met with an overwhelming burst of laughter from both of them, not cold derisive laughter, but the gallows laughter that comes at the realization of troubles shared. The lady at the counter chimed in, "You know that's a foreign language down here!"

"Are you from Greenville?" I asked, trying to smile with them.

"Yes, unfortunately."

"I'm looking for a place to live," I said. "Do you have any suggestions?"

The first lady, Nicki, glanced at the rental-car form and responded, "Well, we just moved down to Riverside." I knew nothing about Riverside, but her posture said it all. It was the same attitude of self-disappointment that I would get later from good students who had let mediocre students copy their work—a knowledge that without actually doing wrong herself, she had let something deeply wrong pass by her without protest. Nicki's quiet penitence bespoke a decency that put me at ease for the rest of the conversation. "We used to live up here in Greenville back when I was pregnant with Josh. . . ."

Nicki went on to tell me that some years ago she was pregnant with her second child and living in Greenville. Although she never told me where, based on her description it must have been one of Greenville's working-class neighborhoods that sociologists would term "in transition." Over the next few days I would find that people in Greenville just call them "turning," meaning "turning black." She was on the front porch of her mother's house, talking to her mother and monitoring her toddler as he sat on the porch. Whatever the demographics of her neighborhood, it was evidently no shock to see a little black boy riding a bicycle on her street; therefore, she paid him no mind. When she turned her back to the street, while reaching over to pick something up for her child, she heard a pop and felt a sharp, deep pain in her backside as she fell to the ground.

As Nicki described it, this boy had been ordered to shoot somebody for initiation to his neighborhood gang. All of nine years old, his tiny hands barely big enough to hold the handlebars of his bike and keep a gun under his shirt at the same time, he had pulled up to Nicki's porch and decided he had found his target. Evidently as shocked as Nicki, the boy dropped his bike and did not move until the police came. She was taken to the hospital and was eventually fine, as was the baby she was carrying. "Luckily, I had some padding," she said with a shy smile. Because he was nine years old, the boy had to wait at Nicki's house while the police called his mother to come to accompany him for questioning.

After that, Nicki and her husband decided it was time to move to Riverside, a white community about twenty miles south of Greenville. From Nicki I learned the fundamental pattern of racial migration in Greenville. The blacks lived north of Highway 82, and the whites lived south of it; as the blacks drifted south, the whites drifted still farther south. However, moving to Riverside was not a subtle migration but a drastic action, like a wealthy man at an auction elevating the price with one unreachable bid. Wary of moving a few blocks farther south every few years to avoid the encroaching black presence, the whites who moved to Riverside decided to make one definitive twenty-mile step.

Nicki informed me that her neighbors had more direct methods of dealing with threats of integration. People on her street had organized a pact such that whenever a black family looked at a vacant house or lot in the area, the neighbors would pool their money and encourage the realtor to accept their false payment in earnest on the lot, then tell the family that, with regrets, the lot had already been taken. Once the family had safely given up and gone looking someplace else, the money was returned and the "For Sale" sign replanted.

Before I left the car rental office, I asked directions to the school. Nicki's coworker told me that it was right down the street that ran behind the building. She said she knew this all too well because the students gathered behind her office to smoke pot before they went to school. She proceeded to play the cards she had been holding so tightly, anxious to add her perspective on Greenville, and as she did I could tell from Nicki's silence that she was a little ashamed of her coworker. The woman told me how "these kids" went to school only to deal drugs, and how she had thought about teaching, had even been a teacher once, but all they wanted over there now were baby-sitters: None of the kids came to learn.

I gathered my papers and the car keys and thanked them both. I was about to turn and leave when Nicki said something I will never forget: "The blacks keep moving into our neighborhoods, and you gotta take sides."

What surprised me was that she delivered her comment with a profound sadness, the way a sister talks to a brother about their parents' divorce, the way we talk about lost friends whom we never truly conceded losing.

Although it was the only open business on South Hinds Street, it was still difficult to locate the small brown sign that read REALTY. I walked into a depressing, dimly lit brown room with a hefty man sitting behind a desk. A stout man with a closely trimmed beard and a soft middle-aged wave in his hair, Sherborn had the face and the long substanceless pauses of a small-town politician. After brief introductions, in which he seemed disinterested, I asked him what properties he had for rent. Sherborn scratched his beard and glanced toward the room behind him.

"We got any friends with carriage houses open right now?" he called out.

A female voice with a soft drawl called back, "What about the Smiths? I think the boy who was staying in their carriage house moved back to Biloxi."

"There you go." Sherborn picked up the phone and dialed. Tilting the receiver, he directed his comments toward me as he waited for an answer: "What we need to do is put you in a carriage house with one of these nice families where you won't have to worry about safety or anything. This other Realtor friend of mine's got one, although he might not give it to me. He's still a little pissed because I sent him some blacks a while back. They were good blacks though. I knew 'em. There are some you know well enough, they probably ain't gonna move in and shoot the place up."

Fortunately, the man he was calling answered the phone and liberated me from making a response.

"Bob," he said, "I got a kid here looking for a carriage house. He looks like a decent kid, doesn't have long hair or earrings or any of that mess. You smoke pot, son?"

I shook my head.

"He don't smoke pot or nothing. Aww, come on, you're not still mad at me about those blacks, are ya? How they doing so far? Well, there ya go, I told you they was good ones." There was a pause as Sherborn listened to his friend's response; then he let out a bellowing laugh and hung up the phone. "Well, turns out he's already rented his to somebody. Sorry, that's the only carriage house I know of. I only got one or two other properties and those are both gonna be too big and out of your price range."

I waited for him to acknowledge that the wall behind his desk was covered with photographs of houses with red tags beneath them that read "For Rent." I picked out one of the photographs behind him that looked attractive and affordable.

"What about that one?" I asked.

He stared at me for a long moment, waiting to see if I would withdraw the question. Reluctantly, he swiveled his chair around to study the wall of photographs behind him.

"Oh yeah, that one," he said, "well, yeah, there's that one if you want it. . . ."

It was as if I had just inquired about a tree house.

"How much is it?"

"Probably around . . . four hundred seventy-five dollars," he said. I asked about another house on the wall and it received the same reaction. I asked for the addresses of the two places so that I could investigate. He obliged, listlessly handed me the keys to both houses, and sent me on my way.

When I found the first address on Havana Street, which was the one that I preferred, I knew I did not need to search for the second, as my assumption had been correct: a black neighborhood. Not even in transition.

The house looked wonderful, so I decided it was time to explore the neighborhood. In Greenville, steps and shade may as well be La-Z-Boys and mai tais, because they are the only requirements for a good gathering place. Under a carport across the street, a group of eight or ten people sat in the shade: some perched on a mother's knee, some crawling, some playing with the scattered debris of toys in the yard, some smoking cigarettes, some drinking from paper bags.

There were at least three grown men and two grown women in the group, and conversation continued through a constantly opening screen door, with some unseen party giving occasional direction from the living room. I turned from the steps of my potential new house and began on a direct line for those shaded steps. Several members of the group had been watching me and continued doing so, still disinterested by the fact that there seemed to be no other place I could be going but toward them. I was across the lawn and under the carport before an uncomfortable silence acknowledged that ignoring me would not make me go away. Fearing the silence, I introduced myself and told them that I was a new teacher at Greenville High. I extended my hand to an older, dignified-looking man wearing a work hat. He looked at my hand as if I were offering him a pile of mud, and then looked away.

I stumbled into a question about the safety of the neighborhood—one that I realized was probably insulting as soon as I had asked it—as a yellow Caprice Classic turned the corner and pulled up the driveway. A woman in her mid-forties stepped out. A girl, perhaps seventeen, got out of the backseat holding a child who could have been her brother or her son. Two other young men, who could have been brothers or boyfriends, emerged from the car. The next few minutes were a constant commotion of passing babies, picking up toddlers, carrying things to and from the car, greeting and drinking, and universally disregarding the strange white boy standing frozen in the middle of the carport. At one point, without yet having been spoken to, I ended up holding a baby and a large toy.

Evidently I had done something, either through my dumb perseverance or my successful handling of the baby and the toy, so that the taciturn gentleman who had at first refused my handshake was reconsidering my qualifications as a neighbor. He gestured toward my house and said something so quietly that it was inaudible. Pleased that he was conceding to talk to me, or even to talk while I was in his presence, I stepped closer to him and asked, "Pardon?" My question did not stop or even delay his sentence, but I was now close enough to hear what he was saying. He spoke in a gentle, deliberate voice, his cadence animated by that distinct Southern lilt I grew to love:

"Yeah, that preacher sho' stayed there. Musta been 'bout two years now. I usta cut dat yard, and dem bushes too. Man damn near tore the place up for a preacher. Now he done got his own church up by Shaw somewheres. Left off to live with his kinfolk. Wife never too much came down here, she always stayed up there with her people. He sho' had some folks living up in there, always somebody comin' and goin', couldn't hardly keep track of the cars. Used to have all sorts of lil'uns over there, always got to throwing stuff up on the ruf, I reckon you got a ruf full of crap up there. Put that cellophane around the windows though. Done right by that."

As he was talking, he was drifting out into the yard and toward the street. By the time he had told me about how exactly he had cut the grass and the wall of shrubs that lined the eastern and southern sides of the front yard, we were standing right next to them. I thanked him for his help and asked him his name. He muttered something about his real name that I could not catch, but said that I could call him "Reb." He looked south down Havana

Street as if measuring something. A block away, a group of meandering boys filled the street with their slouching bodies and boisterous conversation.

"Seven years ago I was the first black to move up into this
neighborhood," he said. "When I moved in white folks wouldn't
even shake my hand. I moved into that house right there." He
pointed across Havana to the south. "I worked every day, come
home every night and had a drink and set right on dat porch and
dat was it. Then dat family down the road up and moved in.
Come a while, mo' and mo' black folk moves in and mo' and mo'
white folk moves out. But they still some white folks that stayed,
and I don't blame 'em none neither. Old white couple lives down
there. 'Nuther white guy and his ma live down that a way and
they don't have no trouble. They wasn't fixing to be run out of
their neighborhood and I got no problem with 'em staying. They
do fine here."

It was only then that I realized he was trying to assuage what
he perceived to be my fear of living in a black neighborhood by
pointing out where the rest of *my people* lived. Anxious to correct
his assumption, I told him that I was not in the least bit worried
about living in a black neighborhood, and left it at that.

"Have you ever had any problem with safety here?" I asked.

Reb smiled amicably and began to diagram the vulnerabili-
ties of my house as if he were defending against an invasion. "You
know ain't nobody coming through that woman's yard."

Immediately behind my house was a very nice brown brick
house with a Lexus in the driveway and what looked like a Mercedes
parked inside the garage. Whether Reb was right or not about the
tenacity of that woman, it seemed clear that she had much more to
defend than I did.

"And you see that porch over there, well that's where I stay,"
Reb continued, pointing to the shotgun house where he had told

me he first moved seven years before. "And you see that one right next to it, well that's where my buddy stay. We gets off work every day at four o'clock, and from four o'clock until when we go to bed we gonna be sitting right there. That's all the safety you need."

I couldn't help but smile. Reb saw it, and for the first time cracked his weathered lips just far enough that I could see his decaying teeth.

Nelson had mentioned that "work was still being done" on the house and that the electricity had not yet been turned on, so I thanked Reb and decided to take a look inside the house before it got dark. I opened the front door and stepped into the front room that I had seen through the window. It was as splendid as I imagined: The walls and ceiling were newly painted white; the wooden floors were undamaged, although still covered with drop cloths; and an entire wall of bookshelves stood perfectly cleaned and painted. Unfortunately, I walked far enough into the kitchen to see that all the appliances had been removed and all the tiles and counters stripped out; the same was true of the bathroom.

I was sufficiently enchanted by the front room and my conversation with Reb that I returned to Nelson and told him I would take the house. Ten days remained before school started, time enough for mc to return to Colorado, gather all my stuff, and return to Greenville in time to move in and have a couple of days to get settled before classes began. I asked Nelson to ensure that the work on the house be completed by the time I returned from Colorado the following Wednesday. Nothing about the process seemed to interest him. He seemed skeptical that this would happen, although he agreed to put the work stipulation in the contract. He tucked my check into the desk and resumed staring at me blankly, waiting for me to leave. As Nelson's door swung closed behind me, I tried not to think about my suspicion that as

I walked toward my rental car Nelson was having a good hard laugh over a joke I didn't get.

My first full day in Greenville had seemed impossibly long, but it had been productive and even successful. To reward myself, I decided to stop in McCormick's Book Inn, a small bookstore that I had noticed during the course of my house hunting. The store was a modest wooden house separated from the road by a deep square gravel driveway and a few rickety wooden steps.

McCormick was a pensive ponytailed man with glasses, knowledgeable and talkative: a perfect find for a curious newcomer. After browsing through the store's Mississippi section for a while, I introduced myself and explained that I was a new teacher looking for a place to live.

"Is it possible to find integrated neighborhoods in Greenville?" I asked.

"Oh yeah, most of 'em are at this point," he responded.

"Where would be a good place to look?"

He spent a couple of minutes describing neighborhoods on the southern half of town, neighborhoods that my bumbling research had determined were predominantly white.

"Where do you live?" I asked as unobtrusively as possible.

"Not too far from here," he said as he gestured around the corner. This put him in a rather wealthy neighborhood. He did not want to be more specific about where he lived and I did not want to be more intrusive, but I could tell he was reluctantly withholding his real opinions.

"Is there still a lot of racial animosity in Greenville?" I asked.

He exhaled at length and let his shoulders drop, taking off his glasses to clean them on his shirt. He gathered his air, straightened his shoulders, adjusted his glasses and looked me in the face. He spoke slowly and carefully, knowing that any careless phrase could be dangerously misconstrued. I have never met a white person from Greenville who spoke of race with more tenderness, precision, or honesty than Mr. McCormick did on that August night.

"You know what some of my neighbors call my street? Congo Lane. Because a lot of the black kids walk down my street every day to get to school and get home from school. A lot of my neighbors think that's very funny. Do I laugh at it? No. Do I tell them that I'm disgusted by their humor? No. I turn and walk away and keep fairly much to myself, and those folks don't much befriend me anymore.

"We live in a pretty nice neighborhood, but we've been there for over twenty years. When we first moved there it wasn't so nice, but there didn't happen to be any blacks in the neighborhood. Now we have a number of black families that live on our street. Sure, there were people who were a little skittish about them moving in when they first arrived, but they've done wonderfully. They like the neighborhood and the neighborhood likes them. Why? Because they share a similar lifestyle. It's not a question of race, it's a question of values.

"I would love to live in a whole city made of people like my two black neighbors, regardless of what color or religion or nationality they were. Would I want to live in the middle of one of these black neighborhoods down here on Clay Street? Absolutely not. Would I want these people from Clay Street to move into my neighborhood and be my neighbors? Absolutely not. Is it because they're black? No! It has nothing to do with them being black; it has to do with what they value and what I value. And I'm not putting a judgment on what their values are. They just happen to be different from my own. But that's not racism. That's just wanting to live your own life. That's the way I look at it. It's not the color of the skin, it's the way people choose to live."

As I heard him say this I wondered if Reb shared McCormick's values. I supposed it depended on the value. Did he work an honest day every day, or did he wear a collared shirt to work? Did he treat people with dignity and respect, or did he make sure that his lawn was mowed? Did he sit on his porch and drink beer from a paper bag, or did he drink it in the privacy of his own home while he watched television? Did he have children out of wedlock, or did he just go to strip clubs when he closed a big deal? Which exactly were the values that mattered? I didn't think to ask McCormick those questions that night, because I believed that—like Nicki—we were living the best answer we could find.

TWO

Whenter I saw it for the first time, Greenville High School was at once something less and something more majestic than I had imagined. It sprawled with the inarticulate design and scope of a major urban high school, yet it was only two stories tall and maintained an ineffable small-town feel. From the front you were convinced that you had reached the back of the building, and from the back you were sure you had reached the back of the building. There was no visible nameplate or entryway. One modest walkway led to four recessed metallic orange doors without windows, tucked defensively under a two-story brick façade.

I arrived early on my first morning to meet the principal and confirm my position before faculty meetings began. When I entered the principal's office, a slender, soft-spoken black man stood up and extended his hand. "Good morning, Mr. Johnston, welcome to Greenville High."

We talked indirectly about the school and its history for several lagging minutes. Like myself, Willie Amos seemed uncomfortable with the idea of having hired me sight unseen, but we also knew that it was far too late to pretend that this was a legitimate interview. After some stumbling about schedules and protocol, I eventually prodded Mr. Amos to admit that I had the position. I breathed a sigh of relief and asked him to show me my classroom.

Room 227 was at the end of the hall on the second floor, the very last room on the right before the annex. The annex was barricaded shut by two enormous steel and wooden doors reinforced with heavy metal chains and a series of bulletproof padlocks. The next week I was told that my room was situated at a dangerous crossroads: directly opposite the second set of stairs that were much narrower and more confined than the expansive ones Mr. Amos and I had climbed. Because my room abutted the annex, the hallway did not extend directly south beyond my room, but turned hard right for about ten yards and then turned back to head south, creating a nook where students could hide without being seen from either side of the building. These two easy exits offered well-traveled escape routes for those who wanted to pull a stunt in front of my room, and then disappear into the annex or down the stairs.

I noticed the brown nameplate that read "227" mounted on the door. Beneath the window was a matching plate that announced "English." The key that Mr. Amos gave me jiggled temperamentally before it caught and turned. I opened the door facing a wall full of dingy, duct-taped windows covered sporadically by dilapidated shades. The shades, backlit with the morning sun, cast long beautiful shadows across the room. The three other walls were covered with chalkboards so scratched, rusted, and embedded with chalk dust that I couldn't read the boards even if I wrote on them with fresh white paint. Crooked rows of old wooden and metal desks stood at pathetic attention before the sturdy wooden desk on my right.

There is more quiet in an empty, dark classroom than anywhere else in the world. It hoards that quiet amid the chaos of the school day, and only when all the students have gone does it lay out a perfect stillness, rich with the marks that the occupants have made. It is dead in the way a boy's room dies when he is no longer a child, a half death: a place that commemorates the lives of those who are now living somewhere else.

For an instant I was overcome with nostalgia as well as optimism, sad for what had gone but hopeful that it might come again. I turned to thank my new boss for finally formalizing my admission to Mississippi and began envisioning ways to bring this landscape to life.

A week later, two days before classes started and a day before faculty meetings, I returned from Colorado with my parents, my pickup truck, and a van full of my things. I was unsettled by the sight of repair trucks in the driveway. I pushed open the front door, not sure that I wanted to see what was on the other side. Instead of progressing, somehow the state of the house had significantly regressed. More rusted pipes and decayed wood filled the kitchen than had previously been there, and there was still no discernible sign that this space was a kitchen at all, or possibly could be. The walls in the living room and the front room were nicely painted and the floors sanded, but the only bathroom was an unspeakable horror. The piping in the bathtub had burst out of the wall like a caged giant freeing itself. There was no sink, only a skinny rusted pipe protruding haplessly from the floor. The toilet consisted of a seat and a rusted cavity, two swollen pipes pushing out of the floor, tilting the commode toward the opposite wall.

Evidently the horror was apparent in my face, because the man who owned the trucks outside spoke to me from the kitchen.

"Nelson just called me onto this job a couple days ago," he said. "There's at least three weeks of work here and I'm short-handed one man."

It was late afternoon and I had to be at school for teachers' meetings the next morning. My parents were waiting outside with a van and a truck full of household goods, and it was now clear that I had no place to put them. My parents had to be back at work in Colorado in three days; I had to begin teaching in two. My sadness at losing the place I loved on Havana Street was subverted by my rising anxiety at having no place to live when school began.

I climbed back in my truck and drove to Nelson's realty office. I wanted my deposit and first month's rent back but feared that I was bound to lose some of the deposit, as I intended to break the lease. Nelson wasn't the least bit bothered with my anger, nor with my plan to break the lease.

"Well, since you are breaking the lease, see, I've already taken the property off the market when you signed that lease, which means I've lost the money I could have made to rent it to somebody else. That's just what that first month's rent is for, in case somebody tries to up and break a lease like you're doing." He sighed deeply, trying to muster a façade of genuine concern. "I guess the only thing I could do for you is keep that first month's rent and put the house back on the market, and if I can still rent it this month, then I'll give you back whatever amount of the rent I didn't lose in that in-between time."

I conceded, knowing he would not give me a better offer.

Something tangible had changed in Nelson's manner after I showed interest in the photos of the houses mounted on the wall behind his head. Had I stayed with a carriage house, I suspect our relationship might have been quite different. A dignified wealthy white woman whom I had met through a mutual friend had suggested I contact Nelson. Since that day, I had been meaning to ask her why she did. Now I realized I had played the wrong card with Nelson. Had I demonstrated a different set of values, he might have taken me in as a surrogate son. As I rose to leave, I recognized a large frame full of Greenville High School paraphernalia mounted in the back of his office. I had told Nelson earlier that I was a new teacher at Greenville High.

"Oh," I said, "you went to Greenville High?"

Nelson looked back coldly. "That ain't the same Greenville High as the one you teaching at."

"No," I said, "I guess it isn't. So I guess you'll be in touch about that check."

"Sure," he said.

I never heard from Nelson.

At my first meeting, the principal's secretary had mentioned that the house next door to hers had a "For Rent" sign posted out front. Now desperate, I called her for the address. Ridge Avenue was shaped like a backward "J" and the house for rent was positioned in the deepest part of the curve. I had driven through the neighborhood earlier and found that two blocks to the west, Ridge Avenue was entirely black. As you drove farther east toward the curl of the "J," the number of black families gently petered out as the number of white ones slowly increased. By the time you reached the house for rent, the easternmost house on Ridge Avenue, there were only three black families out of ten in the loop of the street: Mrs. Jenkins, our secretary, was one of them.

I called the number posted on the paper card in the window and, after two tries, reached a man with a thick and amiable drawl who introduced himself as Wayne. He said he would be happy to meet me at the house as soon as possible.

After my experience with Nelson, I was a bit startled by this new man's accommodating gestures. Thanking him, I told him that I would meet him there. Ten minutes later a shiny white truck turned the corner and pulled up the driveway. A wiry man with short salt-and-pepper hair stepped out. He was in his early fifties, a retired marine who carried himself with a dignity befitting his age and his service. His face was narrow and weathered, his movements spry and direct. As he fiddled with the keys, he informed me that he was still putting on some finishing touches. Fearing that his definition of finishing touches might be the same as Nelson's, I was surprised to see an immaculate house outfitted with brand-new appliances and carpeting: three bedrooms, one bath, full kitchen, dining room, and living room for $450 a month. The decision seemed impossibly easy: At a lower price I would have twice the square footage, functional appliances, and a dignified and responsible landlord. Why, then, was I still profoundly ambivalent?

Wayne leaned his elbows on the front of his truck, and pointed a finger at the sign that listed his phone number in the window.

"You know, I bet I've had thirty-five phone calls in the last three days since I put that sign up and I've returned as many of the phone calls as I can. Just about every family's been black. These people right here in this neighborhood been here about fifty years. They're all good folks, and they all asked me to do my best to make sure I rent the house to someone good, and I know they want somebody white. But it's not just that. Personally I got no problem renting to a black family. Hell, when you been in the Marine Corps as long as I was you can't help but know blacks I love like family. But the neighbors are afraid if I rent this to some nice black family I might come back here six months later and they got their cousins done moved in and maybe an uncle or two down from Chicago, or maybe their daughters got some kids, and before you know it, I got eight, ten, twelve people living in this house. All that means is the rug gets torn down faster, the walls get kicked up by little kids faster, stuff gets broken, the lawn gets cluttered up, broken cars sitting on the lawn. Then they move out and I got to fix it all up again. I mean you're single, you're young, you're a schoolteacher, you're white. I gotta tell you I jumped at it when I got your call."

Wayne sensed my ambivalence because he shared it. He did what honest men do in uncomfortable situations, laying bare the ugly truths along with the flattering ones. Whites had already abandoned the western part of Ridge Avenue and blacks were moving steadily down Elizabeth Street from the north. Should my house fall, whatever short stretch of Ridge Avenue that was still predominantly white—or still shared the same neighborhood "values"—would be penetrated. Like Nicki, I was being asked to take sides.

The door of the next house slammed shut and a white teen-age girl walked out, carrying an infant and leading an angry toddler forcefully by the hand. I glanced up at Mrs. Jenkins's house, stoic and silent. My first class was less than forty-eight hours away and my parents had to unload the van in order to get back to work in Colorado.

I shook Wayne's hand and told him that I would take the house, then hurried off to meet my parents. Although I had succeeded in finding a wonderful house with a responsible landlord in one of Greenville's most integrated neighborhoods, I was disconcerted by the lingering sense that I was now a party to something ignoble. And I had yet to meet my first student.

The next day I arrived at school early enough to explore the facilities before faculty meetings began. The doors to the annex were unchained and turned all the way back so that the building looked a little more like a school and less like a holding chamber. I passed through the doors and turned through the dogleg corner and down the hall. The hallway was dark, except for a twenty-foot stretch in the middle where bands of refracted light seeped in from a row of windows. Opposite these windows, recessed into the wall, were two modest trophy cases. They were the only displays of any kind that adorned the walls on this half of Greenville High School. The trophies were so dusty and rusted that this recess in the wall looked more like a time capsule full of pewter goblets than a functioning trophy case. I bent closer to read some of the inscriptions: "Debate Champions. 1958." In our first meeting Mr. Amos had told me that we did not have a debate team and he could not remember when it fell from existence.

There was a handful of trophies for swimming—another activity that I was sure Greenville did not have anymore—track and field, and baseball. I could not find a date more recent than the 1960s on any of the trophies. Either the school had truly decayed into ignominy since the sixties or someone had lost the key to the case, because it appeared that there wasn't an event we did not win in the sixties, and yet there was not even one that we entered in the three decades that followed. Before I left the annex I turned to the windows that offered the hallway its only light. They looked out at the football field, grand in scope but meager in construction and decor in the way that small-town football fields are. The decaying goalposts faced off against each other in silence.

As I looked out at the field, I tried to imagine the sounds of Friday night laughter and chatter blending with playful squeals as kids ran up and down the bleachers. And then something caught my eye. The windows here were old and rickety like the ones in my classroom; duct tape blended with the steel frames in several places to hold the glass together. Along the bottom row of windows was a perfectly round hole, the circumference of my little finger. Cracks in the glass extended from the circle in the way a child draws rays of sunshine stretching from the sun.

It was undoubtedly a bullet hole: The sides of it were not rough but perfectly smooth, as if it had been cut by a surgeon who grew lazy enough to crack the surrounding glass. I noticed that the hole pointed directly at the trophy case, but when I turned the case was unmarred, and the buildup of dust inside the glass assured that it hadn't been replaced. I searched the wall for signs of a nick or a hole, but the alignment of the windows and the case were perfect. Either the bullet had met some resistance between the window and the case—perhaps a person—or the bullet had not been fired from the outside in, but from the inside out. Neither scenario was comforting.

My watch read 8:04; I was late for my first faculty meeting.

THREE

For nearly eight months I had wondered what the first day of school would be like, the one where I dressed up in the shirt and tie and a legion of adolescent faces entered my room. For the previous months, that image had never failed to excite me; for the forty-eight hours immediately preceding my first class, it elicited nothing less than sheer terror.

When I decided I wanted to teach in Mississippi, I applied to Teach for America, a nonprofit organization that places recent college graduates in areas of the country that have teacher shortages. Despite a summer replete with the advice, training, student teaching and mentoring that Teach for America had given me, my own stubbornness had left me frighteningly unprepared for my first day. Monday was approaching and I was preparing to commit all the cardinal sins of teaching. For starters, I did not have a set of classroom rules. I had made a halfhearted attempt at constructing one but stopped midway. I rationalized that these were high school students—they did not need rules posted like kindergartners. In retrospect, I believe I didn't know how exactly to enforce the rules, and the thought of having to enforce them frightened me only slightly less than the thought of not enforcing them at all. I had been given no curriculum, but I had not yet decided if I would even use the curriculum, when and if the school gave it to me. I simply avoided ominous questions. What should my semester plan look like? My nine-week plan? My four-and-a-half-week plan?

My goal for the first day—and for that unspecified amount of time that it would take for my students and myself to understand our roles—was to devise enough activities to keep the class productive and reasonably silent. Once that could be ensured, I would ascend the ladder of cognitive processes, moving to more complex, more interactive, more entertaining forms of learning. For the moment I wanted to make sure I could keep chaos at bay. There was one major obstacle: the block system. Although I taught only three classes a day, each class was more than one hundred minutes long, nearly the length of a standard motion picture. This was a coincidence that I would later see many teachers use to their advantage.

My lack of preparation marked a precipitous drop from the model lesson I had prepared for my Teach for America interview eight months before. In that interview, each candidate was required to present a model lesson to the group on whatever topic he or she chose. The lesson needed to be less than five minutes in length. I'd had more than a month to prepare. By the time my interview came, I felt confident that I had created a solid presentation on the Harlem Renaissance. I had spent an afternoon in Yale's Art and Architecture Library in order to locate a good picture of Michelangelo's *David* and a photograph of statuesque Marcus Garvey riding in his overadorned open-top car in a Harlem parade. I used the library's oversized copy machine to make large copies of the photographs, and mounted them both on construction paper. Several days later I journeyed to Yale's Sterling Memorial Library to investigate literature on the Italian Renaissance and the Harlem Renaissance. I assembled a small library of references and passed several nights scanning them, enjoying the long stretches when I got lost on tangential topics. Occasionally, before I went to sleep, or when I had a few spare moments, I would juxtapose the notes I had taken with the photographs and organize a short lecture in my head.

By the morning of the interview I was confident that I had a solid understanding of my subject matter and an entertaining approach to teaching it. I knew that I had enough information to conduct a class for ten or even fifteen minutes, and the only difficulty was how to pack that ten-minute presentation into my five-minute time slot. With the exception of a few mishaps due to nervousness, the lesson went reasonably well. With one month of preparation, and continued access to one of the best library systems in the world, I had successfully prepared a ten-minute class. In Greenville, I would have eight hours a night—if I did not eat—with only the smattering of books stacked in boxes in my house as resources, and I was to prepare three hundred minutes of lessons each day.

I was sitting at my desk finishing the seating chart when I heard the bell ring. My muscles contracted and I whirled around to check the door, frantically shuffling papers and books to find some order among things that I had never put in order to begin with. Although first period was to be my conference period, the first day would allow no such convenience. Since the students didn't know what courses they were taking, they would literally be herded from the front door to one of four "holding tanks": ninth grade to the auditorium, tenth grade to the cafeteria, eleventh grade to the gym, twelfth grade to the library. Each teacher reported to the holding tank of his or her homeroom. Each homeroom teacher would stand up at the front of the room and call out the students on his or her list. The students would then line up with that teacher, and the teacher would escort them to their new homeroom, where they would receive their schedules and wait for further instructions. That was the extent of the plan, and it was the ambiguity of "waiting for further instructions" that made me nervous.

I surveyed my room, making sure it was fit for guests before I departed for the cafeteria. I knew that once I left the room there would not be another moment of solitude until the final bell rang, so I loitered, straightening papers, straightening already straightened desks, gazing helplessly at the pathetically barren walls. It was not unlike some good-byes that I remembered, perhaps not as teary as the one when my older brother left for college, or as painful as the last embraces of my college roommates after graduation, but it was the next in the series of poignant good-byes. This time it was fare-well to my romantic notion of what teaching might be.

The third bell rang. I took one last unsatisfied look around, and opened my door to the hallway. I carried my homeroom list, the copies of my students' individual schedules, my grade book and a notebook. The only thing I really needed was the homeroom list—I carried the last three only for security and to gather props that might convince the average student that I was, in fact, a teacher.

The cafeteria was cluttered and claustrophobic when I arrived, but it was calm. It was an unadorned square room with rectangular plastic tables. The tables all ran east to west, and were lined up so closely together that a student could not comfortably get in or out of his chair without bumping into the student seated behind him. The chairs were not connected to the tables the way they were in more efficient cafeterias; instead, they floated rootlessly around the room, where they could be easily tripped over or pushed aside or nudged into the aisle to harass a passerby. For now the room was silent, the teachers milling around disinterestedly, talk-ing among themselves and surveying the tables of waiting students. At first glance there was something disconcerting about the atmo-sphere. I studied the room, transfixed by an image that would never escape: This looked more like a juvenile detention center, or even a prison, than a school. The teachers paced with notebooks in hand, casting eyes toward sections of the room that threatened to become unruly. The students waited in submissive rows to be called out, one by one, to form a line and move—well-guarded—to their next holding tank. None of the teachers spoke to the students, as if signs of fraternity might confuse the inmates.

Certainly history is not forgiving, and whatever melee had accompanied the close of school the preceding year stuck fresh in the minds of the administration, and the circle went unbroken. Students buckled under the weight of negative assumptions; the faculty was bowed by the ghosts of bad memories and worse imaginings. On this first day there was little chance for something new. Instead the atmosphere was permeated by the rotten, inescapable return of something old: the dinner that one had not finished, still waiting as a decaying reminder when one arrives for breakfast.

As I began walking across the cafeteria, a student called out, "Hey, what you teach?" As I started to answer, I was interrupted by the loud squeak of a chair, the rustle of people and their belongings moving quickly out of the way.

"I hope you do step to me you ol' rat!"

I turned quickly to see the girl who had pushed back her chair standing up and calling out to a girl sitting at the next table. As I looked at the girl standing next to me, I wondered how she had ended up in this room. She must have been at least 5'10" and outweighed me by fifty pounds. She was built not with the heaviness that often makes girls encumbered, but with the thickness that gives them power. Another squeak rocked the cafeteria as her adversary stood up to meet the challenge.

"I don't know who you calling rat, trick! You know that boy wouldn't a wanted none a me if he'd a been getting what he needed."

This inspired a chorus of "Ooh"s from the crowd.

Sensing impending chaos, I started moving at the fighters. I was a second too late. The girl next to me flung herself at her opponent with arms flailing, all her height and weight thrown with fitful passion at the opposite table. Fortunately for me, the two rows of students that separated them provided a buffer—she fell into a handful of girls who propped her back up and attempted to restrain her and soothe her seething anger. This was the first time I saw students at Greenville High attempt to break up a fight; it would also be the last. Usually students reacted to a fight the way wrestling fans react when a chair is thrown in the ring, suddenly rising to glimpse the illicit entertainment they had come to see.

I attempted to communicate some cliché about breaking up the fight or stepping back, but the cafeteria was now so replete with catcalls and laughter and hisses that nobody could hear me. Noticing my ineffectiveness, and knowing that nothing breeds disrespect more than ineffectiveness, I felt a mounting urgency to impose a teacher's authority on this situation. I stepped closer and grabbed the first student's arm. Telling her again to break it up, I pulled first gently, then more firmly on her arm, but neither she nor anyone else even turned to acknowledge my presence. I turned to face her, hoping a stern look and some threatening words would awaken her to the fact that she was in a school, with rules and disciplinary actions.

Instead, my sternness was met with a stare so vapid and incensed that I honestly believed she did not see me, or the cafeteria, or the rest of the students, or even perhaps her opponent. The air rang with the pleas and warnings of all her gathered friends, but I was silent, knowing that nothing I could say would seize her attention. There seemed no possible way to ease the hate pumping in her blood or to resuscitate—from this enraged fighter—someone who would read Shakespeare, solve algebraic equations, and study the American Revolution.

Behind the combatants I glimpsed an imposing white man walking toward us; I recognized him from the faculty meetings as one of the football coaches. Nearly six and a half feet tall and of lumbering girth, his movements were unhurried, his voice calm and patient.

"Come on, baby, come on out of there." He placed a hand on her shoulder and repeated himself. All of the students turned to notice him. The aisle had to clear out when he came through, and it was only against his mass that this girl's rage seemed futile, and she let it expire. I looked up at him; he seemed two feet taller than I at that moment, and I felt like I was disappearing into the chaos of students that had stood up to soothe or incite the commotion. I struggled to get back out into the aisle where I could be clearly delineated from the students. I was thankful for the backup, and only then looked around the room to notice that none of the other teachers had moved, but watched me quizzically as if I were committing some laughable but predictable rookie mistake.

I attempted to appear unaffected by the incident. In fact I was less bothered by the incident than by my own powerlessness, and by the students' ability to detect this. As I drifted back toward the wall, the football coach got everyone seated and escorted the young woman out of the cafeteria, where she was picked up by the security guard and taken away.

After he had safely deposited her, he reentered the room and shot me a smile brimming with satisfaction: "Hey green, how's the first day so far?"

I was too flustered to answer.

"You're the new Yankee, huh?"

"No, I'm from Colorado, actually."

"Sure man, whatever. If it ain't Southern it don't count." He chuckled slowly, his stature shaking laboriously. "I'm Coach Pierson, I coach track-and-field and cross-country and help out with football. And every now and then I get around to teaching world history."

"I'm Mike Johnston, I teach English."

"I hear you're my new track coach," Pierson commented.

31

Confused, I responded, "I never ran track in high school, we didn't have a track team."

"That don't matter, didn't you play soccer in college or something?"

"Yeah, but—"

"Well, there you go," Pierson interrupted. "I need an assistant coach. You got the job."

Pierson smiled broadly and put his huge arm around my shoulders. "Welcome aboard, man."

Shortly after the commotion, Principal Amos entered to give his remarks. They were short and uninspiring, mostly emphasizing the dress code that the Greenville Public School District had implemented the previous year: Solid blue or solid white collared shirts must be worn every day, along with khaki or blue slacks. At some point in the previous spring the administration had decided that this uniform was not uniform enough, so they decided to eliminate blue slacks, leaving only a choice between a white or a blue shirt, always accompanied by khaki pants.

After the principal's departure, a man I did not recognize began the process of calling the teachers in alphabetical order up to the microphone. Each teacher read a list of twenty-five or thirty names; six or eight kids sulked slowly to the front of the room and stared at the ground.

Like the students, I tried to size up the faculty members based on their voices, studying the best and worst to find an approach that would ensure that my trip to the microphone would be an impressive first act. I shifted the items I held in my hands as if there were a scientific certainty to be derived from the correct order: grade book, notebook, schedules, roll. That way the students would see the grade book and know I was serious.

"Mr. Davis, come on up and call your homeroom."

But maybe a visible grade book labeled me as uptight—what would I need a grade book for in the cafeteria?

"Ms. Fowler."

Schedules on bottom, notebook, grade book, roll.

"Mr. Johnston."

The schedules on the bottom made it too floppy; notebook on the bottom, grade book, schedules, roll. Yes, notebook visible: prepared but not uptight.

"Mr. Johnston."

Coach Pierson noticed my frantic shuffling and patted me on the back as I walked toward the microphone. "Don't worry, man, you'll do fine."

Doing my best to be authoritative but relaxed, I began: "Jontrell Wells . . . Jolana Gibbs . . . Michael Saloane. . . ."

The list went smoothly, and when I stopped there was a sizable line of young people strung out behind me. I surveyed the crowd, waiting to find any stragglers. Satisfied that they were either not there or not coming, I walked toward the doorway and said, "Let's go."

I had been grappling with three different sets of numbers as if they represented some algorithm that might yield my class size: the state maximum was thirty-three students per class, my classroom held twenty-six desks, and eleven hundred students somehow fit into Greenville High's rather modest-sized building. I finally had been handed my class list the night before the beginning of school. I was fortunate that my second block and my fourth block were rather small, with seventeen and eighteen students, respectively. It was my third block that made me nervous: There were thirty-five names on the third-block list, and I knew that merely keeping order—let alone trying to teach something—would be a challenge. By the time I reached the end of the seating chart cards, I felt as if third block was the only class I taught. Its scope so dwarfed the other two that they almost sank into insignificance.

I agonized over how to start the first day. I yearned to do something expansive, inspiring, profound. I wanted to explain that in my classroom we would seek more than an understanding of prepositional phrases and literary devices, and that we would measure our success by more than the number of chapters we completed or the number of vocabulary words we memorized.

I wanted somehow to put this on my agenda, but it didn't fit easily between the rules of "no chewing gum" and "no talking out of turn," nor did it belong with the explanation of my grading system or the homework schedule, and it was a tad obscure for the first writing assignment. I was already confronted with the classic dilemma of the new teacher: While your creativity moves you to inspire them, your fear forces you to occupy them.

I settled on a reasonable compromise of the two and opened with a quote from Ralph Waldo Emerson. It was one that had moved me in high school and I now had it displayed on my classroom wall. I wrote it on the board and asked all students to copy it into the first page of their notebooks so that each day we would remember the deeper purpose of our work:

> To laugh often and much; to win the respect of intelligent people and the affection of children; to earn the appreciation of honest critics and endure the betrayal of false friends; to appreciate beauty; to find the best in others; to leave the world a bit better, whether by a healthy child, a garden patch or a redeemed social condition; to know even one life has breathed easier because you lived. This is to have succeeded.

Already I was beginning to understand that the meanings in this pithy sentiment, like many of the most important parts of teaching, could not be so insipidly planned, but were nonetheless anxiously awaited. Teaching would not be a simple process of writing ideas down and watching as students ingested them. Instead I would have to immerse myself in the material with a fervor that encouraged students to follow. If the magic of learning appeared for an instant in the rapidly expanding mind of a tenth grader, a teacher counted himself fortunate, not well prepared. Today I was only well prepared, and well prepared for only the most mundane aspects of teaching. The rest I would have to learn, not from my peers but from my students. And I hoped they would teach me in time for me to teach something back.

FOUR

Generations, movements, and events are sometimes captured in a single moment, photograph, speech, or song. My first semester was captured every day in the living work of art that was my third block. I remember the wariness and the shyness that characterized the students of my other two classes that first day, even the first couple of days. But the third block never had a chance at a single moment of sanity, even before it began.

My homeroom had remained in my room for three hours that first day, so the administration decided to skip first and second block. When the bell finally rang, my third block began pouring in before I could even usher the last homeroom student out. They came in clusters, and the clusters followed so closely on top of each other that I lost track as they entered. As I took one girl's name and pointed her to a seat, two more slipped in behind her. When I chased those two to ask them their names, four more bounced through the door. By the time the tardy bell rang, the line to get in my room was still backed up well out into the hallway. Inside, fewer than a handful had actually been seated. The rest shuffled around, heads focused on the desktops like some strange combination of a crowded museum tour and a chaotic Easter egg hunt. To help arrange my seating charts, I had taped an index card to each desk.

Written on each card were the names of that desk's occupant for each block. As students discovered this feature, the names listed on each desk aroused a cacophony of comments, all coming at once from separate locations without any real concern for who was listening.

"Oh my God, Jacky's up in here next block! She know she crazy! And you know she ain't doing no work up in here! And with Pooh Mac sitting right next to her—uh-huh!"

"Hey! Re-Re's up in here second block! And so is Chris Butts! Now that's one stone-cold crazy nigga right there. D'you see that fight he got in up in the cafeteria last year? Four men holding that boy down and he still kicking! They had him down at the alternative school. I don't know what they want bringing him back up here fur, you know he ain't gonna do nothing but fight and act a fool!"

"Ohh . . . that's my boy now. Don't you do my boy that way."

"Toni! Look girl, Corelle's up in here! This block!"

"Don't matter, he ain't never gonna come no way. That boy don't come to school but to get hisself a free lunch and walk the halls and go home again."

"Ain't he a junior?"

"Girl, that boy ain't no junior. He was a junior when my sister graduated two years ago!"

"Then what he doing in sophomore English?"

"Probably fixin' to flunk. Again."

The line outside the door seemed to be growing, the space inside already exhausted. I assigned three students to a work desk in the back of the room, one on a lone chair by a filing cabinet, and two pulled up to the front of my desk. Somehow there were already thirty-six students in my room and two more listed on my roll who had not turned up.

Satisfied that I had admitted everyone from the hall and closed the door, I surveyed the scene of this new class. It reminded me of Jacob Riis' notorious photographs from *How the Other Half*

Lives, evoking images of tiny tenement rooms with six people on a bed, still more sleeping on the floor and draped over chairs and card tables that doubled as dinner tables. I was afraid that if I walked the aisles I'd step on someone. Six students sat in chairs without desks, three students sat on the floor against the back wall, and two were standing in the far corner. Book bags and legs and shoes poured out of every inch of the room. The feeling was intoxicating. I could see it catching momentum in the eyes of my new students: They had anticipated English class and ended up at a slumber party.

The series of characters and experiences that constituted my third block threatened to break my faith in humanity every day. I began earnestly to believe that my position was in fact an untenable one, that my students were every bit as malicious and incorrigible as every pessimist had promised me, and that there was no real chance at success, because what they fiercely wanted was *not* to succeed.

Anthony and Jimmie stopped at the doorway to my classroom before they entered on the first day. Both were struck speechless for a few seconds until Anthony burst out, "I know Jimmie ain't goin' up in the same room I be goin' in."

"Sho' is. Signed up just 'cus folks be telling me, you know Gawa be up in English two again. So I say, that nigga ain't fixin' to cut up without me."

At this point Anthony lost all control of his body. He was hunched over, laughing so hard he was screaming. "Jimmie, we fixin' to clown up in this mug!"

Jimmie responded by shooting Anthony a high five. Apparently the high five, together with the force of the moment's humor, proved too much for Anthony, because it sent him careening onto the floor in the middle of the hallway, rolling back and forth along the floor as he cackled and stomped his feet on the ground. This drew my neighboring teachers into the hallway. They started to intervene until they recognized Anthony and Jimmie.

"Oh Lord, Anthony, I can't believe that boy still in school. Anthony, ain't you paying tuition up here yet? I know you about grown by now," said Ms. Pittman, a twelfth-grade English teacher across the hall.

Anthony quieted to address Ms. Pittman's question with delight.

"No ma'am, ain't nothing but twenty, won't be twenty-one 'til December."

I would soon discover that Anthony, called Gawa by students and teachers, was something of a Greenville legend. Anthony's memories of Greenville High School extended longer than those of most teachers on the faculty; to that extent, he was something of a school historian. Now in his fifth year at Greenville High, Anthony was taking tenth-grade English, but he promised that this would be the year he would graduate. He worked every night at the local rice mill from 8 P.M. until 2 A.M. His job was to clear all machinery of the rat corpses that frequently got entangled in the mechanisms. Each day he came in with a new story—the quantity, size, and internal constitution of the rats always provided some new and horrendous tale from the front line.

Anthony's father and mother were nearly twenty years apart in age; apparently, they had crossed paths scarcely long enough to conceive Anthony. His mother was sixteen when Anthony was born. This in itself was not as phenomenal as the fact that Anthony's mother went on to give birth to fourteen other children. Anthony's father left Greenville a few years after Anthony's birth, but stayed in the Delta. Now that his father was near sixty, Anthony told me, he had thirty-five children scattered around the Delta. I was skeptical, but the story was corroborated by many, most notably Anthony's aunt, who told a fellow teacher, "Now I ain't swearing by no thirty-five, but sure as I'm standing here I bet I could count off twenty-five chilluns living right here in Greenville that I know be sharing the same daddy."

Jimmie seemed to be doing his best to follow in Anthony's father's footsteps. I had barely gotten everyone seated on the second day of class when I walked by Jimmie's desk and noticed his hand buried all the way in the crease of a girl's shorts. Although she had not protested, I was furious.

Jimmie looked calmly at me and said, "Man, you must have a motor up your ass!"

I sent Jimmie to the principal's office. But my efforts were in vain. By Christmas, two students of mine would be pregnant, and both would identify Jimmie as the father.

At Greenville High School, the third block holds a hallowed and hated place among faculty and administration for one reason: It is the lunch block. Due to problems with kids leaving campus, drug use, and fighting, it was decided that the third block would be lengthened, and every third block teacher would personally escort his or her class to lunch, sit with them at lunch, then return them to the classroom. Because the lunchroom seats only 250 students at once, the third block was lengthened to 145 minutes in order to allow all classes to eat.

Lunchtime is the most sacred time of the school day: If lunch was running late, the school waited. If somehow classes were late in arriving to the cafeteria or late in departing, the school waited. If there was ever a special event that caused students to leave campus or return to campus at an odd time, the school waited. If the cafeteria ran out of food in the middle of lunch (which happened frequently), the school waited. As a result, third block did not last the scheduled two hours and twenty-five minutes, but usually two hours and forty-five minutes, and often three hours before the bell finally liberated me.

Third block began at 11:31 and our lunch was scheduled for 11:57. This left me a compact thirty minutes before lunch to ac-

complish some small educational task. However, because the cafeteria could be congested or running late, what actually happened
was that each class waited until a security guard came to knock on
the classroom's window and tell the class it could come to lunch.
This meant that sometimes we would leave close to 11:57; sometimes we would wait until 12:30 or 1:00. Each time a student saw a
security guard pass by the doorway there was a moment of raucous excitement punctuated by an actual knock on the door, or by
the chorus of moans emitted at his passing without knocking.

When the blessed knock did come, students would erupt
from their seats and dash for the door. At that point it was my job
to line them up in an orderly fashion and escort them to the cafeteria. The cafeteria was perhaps a sixty-yard journey down the stairs
and straight down the hall. A line of thirty-seven people packed
tightly and efficiently is perhaps fifteen yards long. Even during
the first days, my line found a way to stretch itself all the way from
the door of my classroom to the entrance to the cafeteria, without any other obvious signs of misbehavior. The students in the
front simply smiled and said they were hungry and eager to get
to lunch; the students in the back said they were tired and didn't
feel so good.

Upon arriving at the cafeteria, two security guards would be
standing outside the cafeteria door. The cafeteria, along with the
gym, was Greenville High's Fort Knox. Although heavily guarded,
a few well-trained mercenaries could penetrate it. Lunch was the
only collateral Greenville High had against the host of children who
showed no interest in education, discipline, or respect. While some
students didn't care if you gave them a zero or detention, or if you
threw them out of the classroom, they all cared about "getting that
meal." As a result, students had to be accompanied by a teacher to
enter the cafeteria. That way, if you were thrown out of your third
block class, or if you cut it altogether, you found yourself in a bit of
a predicament as to how exactly to "get that meal." When we reached

the door of the cafeteria, provided that there were no other classes already waiting, I would greet the security guards, Mr. Brown and Mr. Jordan, and I would step aside and allow those students that were with me "cafeteria clearance." When the last one of my students had entered the cafeteria, I fell into formation and the vault closed behind me.

Once inside, the students would cross to the food line, where they would pick up their trays and move through the short row of sloppy joes, bruised fruit, and applesauce. The cash register offered a keypad where each student punched in his or her number, and the student's name would appear on the attendant's screen along with the charge due. Ninety-five percent of Greenville High students receive federally subsidized free lunches because they come from families that are at or beneath the poverty line. As a result, most students simply punch in their numbers and keep on walking. Other students punch in their numbers and pay the full price of seventy-five cents.

After our twenty minutes for lunch, the group was lined up again outside the cafeteria exit. We were then supposed to complete the last of the third block rituals: the group bathroom trip. There was absolutely no free time allotted to students during the day other than the seven minutes they were allowed between classes. In fact, much of the support for the block system had come from an increased desire among faculty and administration to reduce the amount of free time students had in the halls: The block system allowed for only three class changes instead of six. As a trade-off, each teacher had to escort his or her class to the bathroom immediately after lunch. And so I was forced to drag my straggling line of thirty-seven students back down the hall and up the stairs, and then past my room and down the hall to the bathrooms. At this point the boys and the girls were supposed to discreetly break up and journey to their respective locations, and then ceremoniously return to the line in order to return to the classroom. Then, satisfied and relieved, full of nourishment and ready to focus, the class could return to my room for another 80 to 120 minutes of instruction.

The first day, we made the trip with little incident, with some striated harmony to and from lunch and a disjointed but reasonably successful trip to the bathroom, and we returned to the classroom and accomplished all the lessons I had outlined for that day. It would be the last day that the third block accomplished what I set out for it to do, and the only day that could bear the words "harmony" and "success" in its description.

On some days problems fell like raindrops, relentless and innumerable; on other days they rose like the sun, simple, bold, and undeniable. In the first week they gathered like distant clouds, promising a day so dark that even temperate days winced with coming danger.

Although the class would manage to extend the length of its human serpent all the way from the classroom to the cafeteria en route to lunch, when we took our bathroom trip the line would fracture with the frenetic energy of a kicked anthill. Some students went to the bathroom, some returned to the room, some got a drink of water, while others just stood in the hall, all with ostensibly good reasons for doing so.

One day upon returning from lunch, the stench coming from my classroom was overpowering twenty yards before I reached it. Montel—a student in his third attempt at English II—stood squarely in the doorway and refused to let me in. Someone had taken the chalkboard cleaning spray (whose warning label read: ALLOW ROOM TO AIR OUT THOROUGHLY AFTER CLEANING) and sprayed "Fuck You" in very clear letters across my bulletin board. The smell was incredibly acrid throughout the room and intolerable by my desk. The third block bell rang thirty-five minutes late that day, and when I finally got home I fell asleep on my couch fully clothed at 6 P.M. A week later I canceled the bathroom trip for the rest of the semester. Instead I passed the first thirty minutes after lunch adjudicating individual requests to go to the bathroom, but decided even that was better for my sanity and the school's safety than taking the group bathroom trip.

The spray was only the beginning; the next day, Kim stood up in the middle of my class and proclaimed, "I need a pass to the counselor, so I can get out of here and move to a teacher who knows how to manage his class."

Later that day, when I asked Kim to stop throwing paper at other students, she stood up and yelled again, "I'm sick of this shit, I ain't fixin' to sit my ass up in this fucked-up classroom no more." Then she stormed out.

Five minutes later she barreled back in to get her books. I was standing in the aisle that Kim needed to walk down to get her backpack, and as she tried to walk over me I put my hand out to stop her. She pushed her thick arm through my hand, picked up her books and pushed by me again.

I wrote it all up on a referral form but heard nothing from the administration. Two days later a security guard showed up at my door and told me I was needed in the principal's office. I was called in to listen to Kim and her mother tell the principal how she had arrived home with severe bruises on her arm and chest from where I had grabbed her and hit her in my classroom. I was too dumbfounded to speak, but just stared at Kim as she cradled her thick arm against her side as if it were totally lifeless.

The next day Kim was back in my classroom. I caught her throwing food at the lunch table, and when I asked her to stop she slammed her food on the table.

"Why don't you get the fuck up off me?" she hollered. "I'm so tired of this bullshit I don't even much want to hear whatever it is you got to say to me, so you can just move your little white ass on someplace else, 'cause this girl don't want to hear it!"

Kim's voice had risen steadily as she spoke, and by the time she finished, the whole cafeteria was watching. After the brief moment of silence following her exclamation, the cafeteria broke into cheers and yells and roaring laughter. Fortunately, there was an administrator in the cafeteria who witnessed this event. Three days later Kim transferred to Greenville's other high school.

On the third day of school the English department informed me that I had to attend a conference in Jackson. After leaving detailed outlines for a substitute teacher and an impossible amount of work for each class, I departed for Jackson. It turned out that the conference had been scheduled for another day and somehow this had not been communicated to our school district, or our school district had not communicated it to us. I realized that if I hurried home I could arrive before third block was over. I walked through the front door of the building at 1:15, twenty minutes before class was supposed to end. Once in the door, the first two people I saw were Jimmie and Anthony, who were surprised by the sight of me. Before I could berate them for roaming the halls, they said that the substitute had given them permission to go to the bathroom, and then they strolled casually around the corner—in the opposite direction of the bathroom.

It took a few seconds for students to notice I was standing in the doorway, because I was too shocked to speak. Two games of cards were being played in the front of the room, one on my desk, the other at the rectangular table next to my desk. All the posters that hung on the front wall were missing, and Post-it notes covered the walls, desks, chairs, backpacks, as well as students' foreheads. In the back corner of the room, four boys were huddled around an area they had cleared. I saw the dice bounce across the floor and a pile of money swooped up by an anonymous hand. Next to them a couple of boys and a couple of girls had formed a similar huddle dropping quarters. ("Quarters" is the most elementary form of low-stakes gambling. Someone drops a quarter and the challenger calls out "do" or "don't." If the quarter "do," meaning it lands "heads," the challenger wins the quarter; if the quarter "don't," meaning it lands "tails," the challenger gives a quarter to the person dropping it.)

Between the two sets of gamblers, a large boom box was playing rap music. Against the back wall a girl sat in a boy's lap with her arms draped around him; she giggled as he kissed her neck and ran his hands up her leg. The desks were so scattered—some lay sideways or on their backs—that the room looked more like an ad hoc barricade than a classroom. I figured that the substitute had failed to report to my class until I noticed a heavyset black woman sitting behind the card players at my desk, her legs crossed, reading my copy of *The Old Man and the Sea*. I smelled smoke from somewhere in the room but could not locate it.

"Folks," I announced, "this is over."

There was a mild groan from the room, a sputter of laughs, a few hasty movements of hands and feet. The first thing I wanted to do was get the substitute out of my room. As she walked toward the door I thought for a moment she was going to apologize, but instead she held up my copy of *The Old Man and the Sea*.

"Can I borrow this for the next period I gotta cover? I'll get it back to ya."

I muttered, "Fine," and herded her out the door.

Once she was out in the hallway, I turned to close the door behind her. As I did so, two chalkboard erasers flew past my head and slapped into the lockers in the hallway. I turned quickly and as I walked to the center of the room giving stern directions, the three girls who were covering the room in Post-it notes smiled at the others and walked toward me. They were standing within arm's length when I realized that the rest of the room was moving in response to their lead. The girls pressed closer as a layer of students pressed up behind them, and another behind those. The girls were pushing me back toward the chalkboard, and behind them layers of students pushed forward. When my back was jammed firmly against the chalkboard and the front row of students pressed more and more compactly against me a number of kids started laughing and chanting the rap mantra that was en vogue, "Tear the club up! Tear the club up!"

After a tense thirty seconds or so the crowd eventually relaxed and unpinned me from the chalkboard, still laughing.

Before the period ended I managed to get the desks returned to manageable order, the Post-its removed from most of the walls and desks, the books and supplies on the floor placed in a backpack or on the table at the front of the room. Many of the most significant findings did not appear until the end of the day. That was when I found two brand-new grammar books that had been ripped entirely in half, including the spines; two more books that appeared to be untouched, except that someone had gone through them and ripped out every page number in each book, so both were useless. Another teacher found three of my posters on the walkway outside the school. They had been stuffed through one of the broken windows along the back wall. I found a heap of ashes in the back of the room that used to be a calendar. My stapler, scissors, tape, and pads had been stolen from my desk.

Long after those losses were inventoried, I stayed late into the evening, erasing the words "Fuck Mr. Johnston" from every flat surface in the room.

FIVE

In addition to its present trials, Greenville High School was still haunted by two catastrophes it had witnessed in the previous year; those stories were told and retold by teachers and students alike. The first event began with two girls who brought box cutters to school, small thin razor blades purchased at a hardware store and easily concealed in a purse or a wallet. Laquanda and Jannie had been exchanging words for a couple of days over a boy whom one had lost to the other. They confronted each other at the top of the stairs during the lunch period, each hoping to catch the other unprepared. As Jannie began cursing Laquanda for stealing her man, Laquanda pulled out her box cutter and slashed open Jannie's forearm. Soon both girls were swinging wildly at each other with box cutters, pulling out each other's hair and rolling on the ground. Before security could be notified, the surrounding students exploded into mayhem. Students threw trash cans, books, and desks. One student hit a teacher in the back of the head with a trash can, knocking him to the ground. Friends of the two girls joined in the skirmish, fighting whomever was in the area. By the time security had defused the situation and both girls had been sent to the hospital with severe cuts, the hallways looked like Watts in 1965.

Although it was a catastrophe in the eyes of the administration and a major victory in the eyes of some students, this incident did not damage the school community nearly as much as the one that followed months later.

Whenever students were cutting my third block, I knew there were two areas where they were certain to be: the gym or the auditorium. These were the most problematic areas of the school because they were catchalls for wayward students and usually had insufficient teacher monitoring. There were frequent reports of oral sex and even sexual intercourse in the gymnasium area during the school day, but no one had ever been caught in the act. There were two side dressing rooms and plenty of hidden space behind the bleachers, and the janitors told me that both spots yielded a handful of used condoms each month. There are more than a hundred kids in the gym every period, ten or so playing basketball and the rest doing whatever they want. Four different coaches each hold gym class at the same time on the same basketball court, thereby allowing the school to place up to 150 students in the gym at the same time. There was a student in my homeroom who moved to Texas on the second day of school; in January, when report cards were issued, the school had not taken him off the computers, so his report card was delivered to my room. While he was listed as withdrawn from his other classes, he had received an A for the semester in gym.

The incident that tarnished Greenville High School's reputation across the state took place in the other problematic area, the auditorium. There are so many scheduling problems in each of the two semesters that students are sent to the auditorium in the hundreds to wait for their schedules to be fixed. This often goes on for the first week of each semester, sometimes into the second or third week, when classes are large and teachers few. In this particular semester there were more than a hundred students in the auditorium and no available teachers to monitor them. A number of students had gone to explore the auditorium stage during the wait. One young man convinced a female student to come backstage with him. While hundreds of students sat in the auditorium, the young girl was raped backstage. She tried to press charges, and while the young man acknowledged that the two had sex, no one claimed to have heard her screams or would testify that she had been forced into sex against her will. The case received extensive media attention in the county and statewide. Eventually the girl's court case was thrown out and nothing became of it, other than to fill another chapter of GHS's precipitous decline into chaos.

In my classroom the chaos did not necessarily decline, but over a period of months some vague semblance of rapport began to emerge, and students began to confide in me in a way that I had not anticipated. As they did, I came to see real goodness, but I also saw in their eyes a world corrupted by the adults living around them. Their stories told of men and women who had forsaken them in the midst of a burning city and were now astonished to see that they had emerged, hardened by fire. Like Achilles, they bore only a hidden spot of flesh that betrayed the reality that, underneath, they were vulnerable—they were still children.

In the middle of class one day, Shatanya, an extremely quiet girl in the front row, stood because she wanted to read a journal entry generated by our discussion of Shakespeare's *Julius Caesar.* The journal prompt was titled "Is anything worth killing for?" Shatanya had a serious learning disability that caused her to shy away from sharing in class. Today it did not, and she read a story about how her father had beaten her mother to death when Shatanya was only six years old. She had watched it all from her bedroom, powerless and afraid. She said she had forgiven her father and even visited him several times in jail, though his violence had left her utterly alone.

By the time Shatanya had finished reading, the classroom was as quiet as it would ever be. I stumbled trying to come up with something to say. I was terrified that the class would ridicule her for her vulnerability, and my anxiety rose when I saw a girl in the back open her mouth. She was always the first to throw an insult, and had a knack for picking the barb that dug deepest.

"I'm sorry about your mom," she said, "but that was straight you read that. That take guts right there. I hear what you saying, ain't our place to judge nobody, you just keep on living."

Jennifer's story was even darker, and she could not tell it aloud. She told me after school one day, as I sat with her waiting for her grandfather to come pick her up. When she was very young, Jennifer's father was discovered floating in the Mississippi River, dead from a fractured skull he'd received before landing in the water. As a result, Jennifer had moved to Florida with her mother and her two brothers. When Jennifer was in ninth grade, her mother had begun seeing a man with whom she quickly broke up because, Jennifer said, he grew too possessive. Soon he began telephoning her with threats, and drove by one afternoon and fired three shots into the house.

Luckily no one was injured, but Jennifer's mother called the police to request protection. The police said there was nothing they could do until she could prove he had committed a crime, but that she should call as soon as something occurred. For days her mother was afraid to leave the house, until finally the family ran out of groceries. She realized she had no choice but to walk the two blocks to the grocery store, with Jennifer at her side. The two arrived at the store safely and were rounding the corner to return to their own house when the ex-boyfriend jumped out of the bushes with a gasoline can. As Jennifer screamed, the man covered her mother with gasoline and set her on fire in the middle of the street.

By the time Jennifer called the police to tell them that something had indeed happened, her mother was dead.

*   *   *

Third block was not my only problem. Chris was in my second-block class; he had spent the previous year in the alternative school and most of the preceding summer in jail on charges of homicide. It was widely believed that Chris had shot and killed a fellow student, but in return for his testimony against an older accomplice, Chris had been released. I had witnessed the fight that led to Chris's most recent suspension two weeks earlier. He had thrown himself across a table at the wide receiver on the football team because Chris didn't like the way he was looking at him. Although the boy had six inches and seventy-five pounds on him, Chris had fought admirably and defiantly, as it took three security guards and two teachers to finally drag him to the principal's office. Although the fight had resulted in only a five-day suspension, it had been more than two weeks since Chris had last attended my English II class. Over those two weeks, I had begun to believe—to hope—that Chris was not coming back at all. Instead, he chose to show up on the day I was giving my first test.

His narrow eyes surveyed the room as he entered, casting a broad smile at all assembled. Chris was only 5'6" and no more than 130 pounds, but the anger he so visibly carried made his presence that of a large and dangerous man. Chris slid into his seat and picked up where he left off the last time he was in my room, harassing the two girls seated on either side of him. "What we doing up in here today? I know you got these folks working, but that don't matter none, 'cause I be getting all my answers right off Shonte here, ain't that right, Shonte? But don't worry Mr. J., 'cause I be giving her something too!"

The boys laughed, the girls smacked their tongues against their teeth and waved a dismissive hand at Chris, while Shonte blushed and stared at her desk.

I informed Chris that we were taking the unit test today, but I would be glad to assist him in reviewing the sections he missed.

"Nah, bump that. I ain't got no time for review. Just give me that test. If all these rockheads up in here can take that test, I know I can pass it."

I managed to get Chris moved to a table by himself, and after I had passed out everyone's test, I tried to explain to him what the test covered. For the first fifteen minutes he worked diligently, quickly answering the questions he knew and skipping the ones he didn't. It was only after he returned to the ones he didn't know that the trouble began. I had watched Chris nestle a copy of our grammar book and *The Catcher in the Rye* under his seat, and now he began the work of perusing them discreetly. I knew there must have been a way to handle the situation effectively, but even now I don't know what it might have been.

I eased over to Chris's desk and whispered, "Remember, even though you've been gone for a while, this isn't an open-book test, so just put down all the things you know and don't worry about the information you missed. I can't possibly expect you to know it all."

"Who you calling a cheater?" Chris hollered indignantly. "I ain't cheating. This man over here trying to tell me I'm cheating out of a book. I don't know who you think you're playing wit', but you best get up out of my face and walk right back to where you was befo'!"

The whole class watched as I withdrew from Chris's desk the way a man sidles slowly from a bomb he is not sure has been defused.

I tried whispering one more time, "Chris, I didn't say you were cheating. I was just encouraging you to answer the questions you knew and leave blank the ones you don't know."

"You think I'm stupid? You don't think I know what cheating is? You don't think I know what you trying to say? Don't try to change ya' story now, I know what you said. You told me to quit cheating out the book, and I tell you I ain't cheating out of no damn book. What I need a book for? You must think I don't know this easy shit, I could do this with my eyes closed."

Now the students had put their pencils down. Chris knew he had a captive audience.

"Chris, why don't we step outside and we'll talk about the test while these people finish up work. Okay, let's not worry about the test. Let's just—"

"Oh, you saying I flunked now. You saying you gonna take my test for cheating? Well, fuck that!"

Chris pushed back violently from his chair and threw the two books he had hidden in his hands across the room. The grammar book slapped against the blackboard and the pages slithered out of their yellow spine. The paperback novel struck Shonte in the side of the head.

"Chris, that's it. Out of the room right now before I have to call security."

"Before you have to call security? Call fuckin' security, these folks think somebody afraid of those sorry security guards. Man, you just don't know, those security guards ain't nothing but some punks. What they carrying? Nothing but a fuckin' radio. You got to step to me with something better than a radio if you think I'm fixing to back up."

"Chris, it's your first day back, and you know they're going to put you in the alternative school if you pull this again."

"Man . . . principal, alternative school, disciplinary hearing, so fuckin' what? These folks playing. I been to the big house and made it just fine. Man, Carver Circle Posse got my back all over that joint. Y'all ain't got nothing more to scare me with, I done seen the worst of it. Man, fuck this whole place! Fuck all y'all!"

He picked up a stack of five literature books sitting at the end of the table and hurled them across the room. Two books landed on empty desks with enough force that they knocked the desks to the ground; one struck a student desk, knocking her backpack and her test into the aisle, and two stray books hit Shashimoree and Nicole.

"Nicole, go get security," I ordered.

Chris paced frenetically during the minutes it took Nicole to return with two security guards. As Chris delivered a steady stream of expletives and overturned two more desks, the class sat silently, frozen between fascination and fear. When the security guards arrived at the door, Chris walked straight toward them, not with the penitence of the convicted, but with the anger of a challenger seeking his next prey. When he was out the door, I closed it and tried to refocus the class. For a few minutes I could still hear Chris cursing in the hallway, hurling threats at opponents I could not see.

Twenty minutes later a security guard returned to summon me to the front office. I made it just in time to see Chris, in handcuffs, tucked into the backseat of a police car. He had attacked a security guard and verbally threatened the assistant principal after he left my room. Later that afternoon the assistant principal informed me that the school would be pressing charges and they needed me to testify. In the meantime the school had obtained a restraining order to ensure that Chris came nowhere near the campus until a formal hearing.

I had volunteered to chaperone the dance after the football game that same night. By the time the dance started, one teacher had been beaten up in the parking lot and two others had subsequently refused to come in to the dance. I was one of two remaining chaperones. The kids complained that there were not enough dances, but because dances were such catalysts of violence, the faculty complained if there were any at all. Once the dance was under way, the only visible threat to safety I could see was the sizable crowd of male students who were dancing aggressively in one corner of the floor. I walked around the dimly lit borders of the darkened high school gymnasium and watched this posse from beneath the bleachers. Its singular mass shifted effortlessly toward the center of the floor. As it did so a single boy popped out of the mix and stumbled toward me. He was within arm's distance when he picked his head up and shot me a mischievous grin.

"Hello, Chris," I said, "I didn't expect to see you here."

"I bet you didn't. That's awright, you ain't been here long. You'll learn." Chris disappeared back into the horde of dancing students and I never saw him again.

Unfortunately, the Greenville High School staff was sometimes guilty of the same opprobrious behavior. Mr. Chandler, one of the school counselors, seemed ebullient and competent at our first staff meeting. Most black faculty members regarded me with some trepidation when we first met, but Mr. Chandler was different. Though in his early forties, he was still brimming with a young man's passions. He flirted with all the women, joked with the men, acted businesslike with administrators. He seemed to have a soft spot for the school's roughnecks, something I admired at first. He seemed always to be returning a student to class, fixing a troubled child's schedule, taking unproductive students out of class to give them a pep talk. For some months that was as much as I knew about Mr. Chandler.

Then one day Larry, a student in my third block, got into a fight in the lunchroom. I quickly wrote the referral and was going to take him to the office myself, but was afraid my class would scatter through the building while I was gone. I saw Mr. Chandler walking down the hall and asked him to take Larry to Mr. Hudson, the assistant principal in charge of discipline. Larry did not return to class that day so I assumed he had been suspended.

At the time, Greenville High School's most popular form of discipline was the zero-day suspension. A zero-day suspension was not a suspension at all but required a student to be accompanied by a parent when he or she returned to school the next day. When student and parent arrived at school, they would meet with Mr. Hudson and the zero-day suspension would be resolved. Any student who was suspended also had to return to school with a parent on the first day back. In a school of eleven hundred students it was easy to lose track of who had been suspended and who was required to show up with a parent for a conference with Mr. Hudson. Most students threw their suspensions in the trash, never told their parents, and returned to school the next day. The "Do Not Admit" list, GHS's version of "America's Most Wanted," was designed to prevent this from happening. This list was a compilation of all the students who were suspended and pending clearance from Mr. Hudson.

Larry did return to class the next day, and his name was not on the "Do Not Admit" list. I was frustrated that Mr. Hudson had apparently done nothing about Larry's fight; usually a fight meant an automatic three-day suspension. I went to see him that afternoon. Mr. Hudson told me he had never seen Larry. When I found Mr. Chandler, he told me he had had a talk with Larry, and agreed to tear up the referral and let Larry stay with him for third block, if Larry said he would not repeat his behavior. From then on I never accepted a pass from Mr. Chandler, and never let a student leave class to meet with him.

Rumors about Mr. Chandler spread with vigor. Within weeks rumors turned into facts and he was on the front page of the Greenville paper. Mr. Chandler had had a serious drug problem for several years. One student I knew well, a family friend of his, later told me that several times a week he asked her to drive him back and forth to various drug houses and drug dealers. But Mr. Chandler's habit quickly outran his income, and early in his first semester at Greenville he had begun selling grades to students. As school counselor, he had special access to all student records and files. Long after a student had failed, he or she could pay Chandler $75 for a half-credit course, or $150 for a full-credit course, and the credit magically appeared on the student's transcript.

Two things brought down Mr. Chandler's otherwise ingenious operation, and only after he had collected several thousand dollars worth of grades. His first mistake was that he had changed the grades on the computer, but not on the actual paper transcripts in the files. As a result, counselors, teachers, and students began en-countering disparities in records. His second mistake was fatal. Certain students who were negligent in passing their courses also proved negligent in paying for those grades, and Mr. Chandler hounded his clients incessantly, even calling home to speak to their parents. The operation crumbled when two parents, thankful but slightly confused, called the superintendent's office to ask whom they should make the check out to for their son's grades. Added to the fact that Mr. Chandler was facing charges for assaulting another teacher outside the lunchroom, he was finally removed amid the scandal. Mr. Chandler was finally removed amid the scandal and transferred to a new position at the alternative school.

Only much later did I see those first few days for what they actu-ally were: an evaluation. My third block students spent the first day casing their target like a sophisticated group of bank robbers who arrive some days before a job to identify the location of the cam-eras, the placement of the guards, the accessibility of the safe, the exact rotation of the staff. So perfectly had they done their job, so vulnerable was the establishment, so large were their numbers, that they knew success was a mathematical certainty, and they swag-gered through the first week with that comfort. What might have taken weeks or months to plan was ready in days. Now they only waited for the sign, not yet sure of who would send it, but fully aware that they would know it when it came.

It would come in the form of a six-foot, nineteen-year-old showman named Corelle Wright. He was one of the two students who had graced me with his absence on the first day, as well as on the two following days. Much later, when I found myself diagnosing the wreckage of my third block, Corelle resembled my twentieth-century male version of Pandora. His charisma, humor, and wit seemed an encouraging gift—but the stock of distractions, dilemmas, curses, fights, tears, tribulations, and nonsense that he carried seemed at times certain to undo us all.

In the Greek myth, Pandora's box included one thing capable of counteracting all the evils it carried: Hope. After Corelle's arrival to the third block, Hope absconded immediately and hid her majestic head for a long, long time. Each day when the students had gone I spent hours searching for her myself, and many days I was certain that her inclusion in the box had been the real myth, handed down to help us tolerate the most desperate moments with some imaginary optimism. It was only months later, in ephemeral flashes, that I began to see glimpses of Hope around the room, sometimes even from Corelle himself. But I would have to pull all the noxious tragedies out of that box before I would find Hope buried at the bottom.

Part Two

THOSE WHO DON'T KNOW

ANY BETTER

Those who don't know any better
come into our neighborhood
scared as a dying man, which is
something I've never understood

Those who don't know any better
think that they have to run.
They're scared we'll stick them with our shiny knives
or shoot them with our loaded guns.

I figure these folks are just stupid.
Yeah! Like some Wal-mart mannequin.
I guess they're lost or here by mistake.
I pray no more reach this land.

But we're not afraid of anybody.
We know the crooked-eye boy is Davey, Baby's brother
and the one next to him is Eddie V.
Because Rosa is his mother.

—ASTRID BUTTS, GHS '01

SIX

It was on a Thursday, the fourth day of class, that Corelle arrived, and twenty minutes late at that. Although I had not yet survived the first week, a lifetime had already passed in that classroom before Corelle's entrance. My third-block class was already slipping irretrievably into chaos ten minutes before lunch. Each day the students pressed a little bit further against the elastic boundary of my authority like water filling a balloon. As I checked my watch to see if I could possibly hold on until lunch, the room was pulsing on the cusp of eruption.

I had prepared a short grammar exercise for the students to complete before lunch, but I still lacked the wisdom to assign a time period in which to complete it. I had managed to obtain one extra desk from a teacher next door and two extra chairs, so at least students were not still sitting on the floor. Nonetheless, my roll held steady at thirty-seven, a solid four students above the state limit. A child or his or her debris occupied every open space.

Since there was no central exercise, I had to monitor progress individually. As soon as I stopped to check on one student, I lost the student behind me; as soon as I had quieted one section of the room, another section erupted. I felt the hopelessness of a child playing keep-away with older boys. He tries to predict where the ball will go next, always arriving too late, driving all his anger and hope into the conviction that if he just runs hard enough he might catch it.

As I surveyed the room I heard a loud thump coming from the door, and noticed a face pressed foolishly against the glass. In the first four days I had already seen enough to know that this was a popular trick, made better for the perpetrator by the fact that it was very difficult to defend against. My tormentors liked to throw themselves or their friends against my door's glass square, then smush their faces as ridiculously as possible against the glass in order to exaggerate the fly-on-the-windshield look. The face then slid dramatically down the window and out of sight. It was a high-percentage trick—always sure to get a classroom full of laughter, always sure of an expedient and anonymous getaway.

This time, however, the fly was not moving, but remained stuck in the middle of my windshield. This was a new variation of the trick: How long can you stay on the windshield before the driver comes to wipe you off? Sensing the mounting laughter, I made quickly for the door. As I got close enough to discern the pieces of the smushed face, I could see that whoever this was, he was not the least bit concerned about my approach. When I stopped in front of the door the face propped itself up energetically. When the person rose to full height he was a full three inches taller than I was, and with a wry smile he tilted his head back to look down his nose at me through his barely open eyes. At the sight of his face two of the girls behind me erupted in laughter.

Without removing his face from the glass, he opened his eyes and a wide grin spread beneath his mustache. Convinced that this was a still braver breed of the same jokester, I mustered a halfhearted command to vacate my doorway.

He slapped a piece of paper against the window and said, "I just came from court."

Behind me, a chain of whispers chased a legion of chuckles. I glanced at the paper he pressed against the window. I saw the seal of the Washington County Courthouse and the name Corelle Wright printed on the top. Corelle Wright, why did that sound familiar?

A voice in the back of the room anticipated my concern: "He's up in here! I know 'cause I'm sitting at his desk."

Corelle Wright was one of the two names that had been absent on my roll for the last three days. I stared back at the court order, searching for charges. . . . "Assault." Corelle's entrance was turning into more and more of a spectacle, so I had no choice but to fully open the door. Corelle stumbled in as if the door had been pulled out from under him. After the first round of laughter, he stopped, straightened, and gave a wave to the entire room. I turned to close the door but it hit something solid. As I turned I found myself looking directly into someone's neck. From someplace behind Corelle his partner had appeared. This student was 6'6", and as wide and dense as two solid men. While standing next to Corelle made me feel small, I watched his laconic sidekick walk past me and stand behind Corelle and suddenly Corelle appeared every bit the twelve-year-old boy that he was acting.

The second student was not overweight, but made of an insulated thickness like artificial turf: a layer of padding endorsed by unforgiving stone. There was something shy in this second boy's aspect, something that did not like the spotlight Corelle demanded, and yet envied Corelle's ability to attract it. While Corelle was entertaining, his partner turned back toward me. He held his head at a downward tilt in an unconscious effort to reduce his height. His eyes were large and extremely bloodshot; they did not focus on me but darted back and forth to either side of me.

"Marcus Walker." He said it with a slight lilt, half rap, half whisper.

At that moment I noticed how awkwardly he moved in his body, as he wiggled and shrugged in futile attempts to hide its size. Corelle Wright and Marcus Walker were the last two guests at this festival of the absurd, and with their arrival everyone knew that the revelry could begin in earnest. I knew right away that Corelle and Marcus would push the third block over the precipice; all that remained was to see how much of the class I could salvage after the fall.

I tried to regain the center of attention by telling them both to sit down, and as I searched for a place to put them I began perfunctorily reciting the assignment. Corelle turned to confront me. Corelle was lost and found in his voice—it could be as vibrant as a mountain summer or as dead as a Mississippi winter, never hateful, but often filled with a distant disinterest, cut with a twist of humor.

"How old are you?" he said. "I bet you ain't but twenty-three, twenty-four. You ain't but a few years older than me, hell, you ain't as old as my brother, and I'm supposed to call you mister. How old are you anyways?"

Only then did I think of the birth date printed on his court order: 1977. He was twenty years old: only two years younger than I was. I asked him to sit down a second time, doing my best to dodge the question, momentarily forgetting that there was no place to sit. I directed him toward an open spot on the floor and much to my surprise he sat down, calling to his pack of fans through loud whispers and blown kisses. As he sat down he smiled at me—not a malicious smile, nor an intimidating one, but an openly friendly one. By the time I calmed the room's reaction to Corelle, we were off to lunch. Between the shouts and detention threats I used to limit my line to one hundred feet in length, I decided that I liked Corelle, and suspected that if any hope remained for this class, it must first go through Corelle.

Thirty minutes after we returned from lunch Corelle was absolutely incorrigible, draping both arms around any girl within reach and talking full-voiced to her about the kind of loving he could offer if she would be his "Boo." Most of the girls feigned objection but smiled continuously, although some did not object at all and even snapped at me when I tried to stop it.

In the first few days, I had established a system of punishments and rewards called "The Three T's: On Time, On Task, and On Target." For each infraction of one of these rules I subtracted five of the "3T" bonus points, with three detractions in one day leading to an automatic detention. Corelle had spent his three strikes in the first five minutes, and I was reluctant to issue him detention when I knew his reaction would disrupt the class even more than the intolerable racket he was making already.

As the volume of his conversation overtook my lecture I could feel the attention disintegrating: Two heads were down on desks, three boys in the back of the room were talking, two girls and a boy were stealing each other's pencils and backpacks. I desperately needed a last stand and knew it had to begin with Corelle.

"Corelle," I said, "that's it. You've got detention."

I crossed to the desk to fill out the detention form.

"You can write out whatever you want," he said, "but I ain't going to no detention, I gotta go to work."

This was a customary response, and I had developed a knee-jerk retort that was equally unhelpful.

"Well, you should have thought of that before you started behaving like a child."

Before I realized that I was pulling Corelle into a battle of wits that I might not win, he turned his chair around from his latest love, and looked straight at me, "Hey, Mr. J., you going to buy my booze for me? You gonna buy my dope? You gonna pay to take my girlfriend out Friday night? You gonna buy those good condoms for me? If you can't do that, I ain't coming to no detention."

The class was in an uproar, laughing and hollering and slapping on desks: Corelle grinned and turned back to his lady, glowing in victory. I continued writing the detention slip but knew, based on Corelle's somewhat convincing speech, that it would be useless. Suddenly I caught sight of the class roll and was taken with a better idea. I scanned the paper for Corelle's name and followed my finger across the page: 322 Russell Street. I endured the eighty minutes of chaos that followed Corelle's trenchant comment, fueled only by the hope that I might have happened upon a panacea for my third-block troubles: I was going to see Corelle's mom.

Corelle was my first home visit. It was only my fifth day of school, but perhaps I should have expected that someone like Corelle would demand my first home visit. The yard of his house was without a blade of grass and its dust had risen and settled on the white wooden house so many times that the two had grown to a muted similarity. Dilapidated stairs spilled off from a screen door that had long been without a spring. In the yard, two boys gestured with the combination of listlessness and sporadic energy that marked so much of my students' casual conversation. I thought both boys were students at the high school, though I had no idea how old they were. I parked my truck next to them and got out. From the moment they saw my face the lively conversation abruptly ceased. I introduced myself and told them that I was looking for Corelle. One of the boys told me that Corelle was at work and would not be home for some time. After some prodding I discovered that both boys were Corelle's brothers.

It turned out that the one standing was Corelle's older brother, who was supposed to be a senior at Greenville High but had not yet shown up for school. He had been thrown out of school the year before for fighting, and had yet to reenroll. I later found out that his little brother, who seemed soft-spoken, was not enrolled in junior high because he had received a year's expulsion for threatening a teacher. They told me that their mother was over at their grandfather's house since he had recently passed away, but they said I could go in and talk to David, their mother's boyfriend. I decided to tell him that I had stopped by, in case Corelle's brothers were moved by brotherly solidarity to forget to mention my visit.

A large, sternly built man answered my knock on the door. David's athletic build and his face suggested that he was not over thirty, but the miles written across his eyes promised that he had seen too much to be so young. He filled the entire doorway, and parted his lips enough to show that he was missing several teeth. It was not until his initial skepticism gave way to moderate interest that he moved enough to indicate that I might pass inside.

The door opened to only one room that exhaled an unnamed smell. It was not the smell of a cheap cleaning product or low-quality preservative, no particular human or animal stench: It was the smell of an absence. It came from the absence of a dishwasher and the absence of a biweekly trash pickup, from the absence of clean water and meals cooked with fresh ingredients, from the conservation of food not meant to be preserved, from shoes worn without socks.

A card table stood in the center of the room. Behind it were two shelves that constituted the kitchen; to the left a torn-up recliner faced a corner full of knickknacks that indicated a sitting area. David's concern for Corelle seemed to increase with my stay. He was in the middle of taking my phone number and promising to take away Corelle's car when Corelle's mother walked through the doorway. She was thrilled that I had come; it was obvious that I was the first teacher ever to visit the house. She was quick to condemn Corelle before I even started speaking, beginning a tirade about how hardheaded he was, how he refused to "get his lesson," how many times she had told him about studying and minding his teachers, and how quickly she would get on him.

She showered me with compliments, remarking at how young I was, and how impressed she was that I had come by on Corelle's behalf. "Shoo', Corelle ain't had a teacher call me or talk to me since el'ment'ry school," she said. "Das the problem, ain't nobody care no mo', dat's what he need, he need somebody like you who gonna stay on him, make sure he do right and get his lesson. I tell ya this sho' as I'm sitting here, he a had some more of you way back when, he sho' wouldn't be acting a fool the way he is now. Dat's a truth too, they need more teachers like you up over there."

Five minutes of our conversation had passed before I realized that Corelle's mother was high on marijuana. Her eyes looked like Marcus Walker's had that morning—bloodshot and unable to focus—her movements slowed as if underwater, her laughter was sporadic and irrelevant. It struck like a powerful blow, taking my air for a couple of minutes and leaving me listless and defenseless. Fortunately she did not stop speaking long enough to expect any response from me, so my recovery went unnoticed. It was her tirade on morality that cleared my clogged head like a muted television whose volume is suddenly restored.

"'At's what I always tells my kids, don't be stealing, don't ever steal nothing. Jus' ain't no sense in it. If you need sump'n, den ya ax for it, don't go stealing fuh nothing, cause you sho' bound to get in trouble. That's why I tell 'em, I says if you want some dope, ax me! Don't go stealing from somebody down in the park to buy it. Don' go jumping on some crackhead or little children to take no money for dope. If I gots some dope, I'm gonna share it with you, and if you gots some I expect you to share it with me. But that ain't no call to go stealing, cause stealing ain't right nohow."

I wanted badly to leave Russell Street, knowing that the longer I remained, the more intractable Corelle's situation looked, and the deeper I immersed myself in the most heartbreaking of stereotypes. I guided the conversation toward a conclusion, neglecting the careful steps I had planned for securing open lines of communication. I had come upon a problem much larger than one requiring a periodic phone call home. Followed by a chorus of thanks, I made it to the door, where Corelle's mother told me for the third time that if all of Corelle'e teachers were like me, he never would have turned out this way. That struck me as almost more disturbing than the first statement. She knew that Corelle was in trouble; in fact, she considered him worse off than that. In her eyes Corelle's case was terminal and irrevocable; she was left only the job of anesthetizing his gradual departure. The screen door slapped shut and I stumbled into the dirt yard. I nodded to Corelle's brothers, too disheartened to be diplomatic, and climbed into my truck.

My stomach was still dropping when I rounded the corner and started down the street adjacent to Hardy Park. I noticed a gathering of kids on a bench not far off the road, and as I passed I nodded to them. Seconds later two or three of the group got up and started running after my truck. Most of the group consisted of women, even young girls, and I wasn't panicked. Most of the runners petered out like falling stars, but the last runner showed no sign of slowing, and as she closed on my truck I could see the look of horror that moved across her face. I stopped the truck, rolled down my window and let her catch up to me. She stumbled to my door with the loping strides of a sprinter after she has crossed the finish line. The dark face stopped at my window and did not speak. She looked much older now than I had thought. After a long pause she began stuttering, "What da you . . . where da you want the people to go . . . can I have a sucker. . . ." She rambled like a toddler too overwhelmed with the complexity of things to focus on any one thing for any one instant. Then her eyes flashed and the child was suddenly gone. "I'll do anything—I just— whatever you got, a few bucks can get me just . . . I'll get in there with ya. . . ."

She started drifting backward as if the car were pulling away, though my foot was firmly on the brake. She began drifting still faster, as if the terror of things pulled her with greater and greater force backward toward the park, toward her partners who watched from where they stood, hovering like scattered leaves after a swift wind.

Before I could think to give her some money, or ask her if I could help, she was gone, tumbling backward and then running back to the group from which she came. I watched the girls rustle and stir into a pile, the last leaf tumbling slowly back. I released the brake and eased slowly away from the park and down California Street, looking into the eyes of each person lounging on each porch, feeling them look back. First an old woman, than a group of younger boys, than an old man and woman together; each pair of eyes reflected the same thing: a sadness hardened over with acceptance, a longing dwarfed by a knowing.

The blank stare I received from those faces was a mixed acknowledgment, a defiant protest against my desire to make categories where they might not exist. But buried beneath those stern glares was an embittered wish for a world where a man's goodness and badness might stand alone as the variables determining his worth, a wish that even the most impossible circumstances might afford some hope.

It was just two days later that Corelle was again so disruptive in class that I had to put him out in the hall. It was the first time as a teacher that I felt truly angry. Up to that point, anger had never emerged—I had felt only frustration and despair. The anger was due not only to Corelle's misbehavior, but also to the fact that I had invested so much in Corelle and he seemed impervious to it. When I stormed out into the hall where he stood waiting, I did not stop to think about the tone of my voice or the nuances of my phrasing; I simply aired my consuming disappointment and spared no sentiment in doing so.

When I finished, Corelle stood silently. I was able to hear the pulse of blood running in my head, and feel the tingling of adrenaline in my fingertips. I had almost forgotten the feeling of wanting something so badly that no excuse was tolerated. My hopes for Corelle had transformed frustration into a curious and all-consuming dedication to a single goal: helping Corelle succeed. I had crossed the threshold and become a teacher. I had found my first true student: A few inches taller than I and two years younger, his was not the face I had expected to adopt, but so it was.

My faith in Corelle had not yet returned enough to allow him back in the room. The day was already a catastrophe: Even the quiet kids were busy passing notes, stealing each other's notebooks, and painting their fingernails. I would be hard-pressed to regain the reins even without Corelle present. I instructed him to wait at the doorway for five minutes until he was ready to come back in and work in peace. I returned to the melee inside and did my best to channel its fervor into some discussion of *Julius Caesar*. Ten minutes passed in a chaotic blur. Then I remembered Corelle and walked toward the door. Looking through the glass in my door, I could see that he had disappeared. My stomach dropped. But my anger could last only as long as those brief moments between uprisings, and before I could absorb yet another defeat from the incorrigible Corelle, the circus was heaving and lumbering into motion, and I was off to position myself precariously at its head.

For six months, the bell that signaled the end of third block was my personal salvation. Each day its arrival was a new miracle—a miracle some days three hours in coming, but a miracle nonetheless. When the bell finally rang on this particular day, I opened the door and, stepping into the hall with the flow of students, nearly tripped over Corelle. He was seated against the wall. He raised his head and stared blankly at me. Still upset, I asked him where he had been.

"I been right here, waiting for you."

Later that afternoon I found Mr. Jordan, a security guard who knew Corelle well. Mr. Jordan had kept a close eye on him during third block: For two hours he had watched Corelle sit silently outside my door.

A few days later, as I walked out of the lunchroom I ran into Corelle and his sidekick, Marcus. They had cut my class and both were obviously high. Before I could find security guards to take them to the principal's office, they offered some advice about their grades.

"Now don't be making no enemies come grade time, Mr. J., 'cause you know this town be too small to be making enemies," Corelle said. "In a town where everybody be knowing where you stay and what kind of beat-up blue Ford Ranger you drive, you don't want to be making no enemies. Sheeet, you ain't but a year or two older than me no way, ain't like it'd be doing in an old lady or nothing. Be just like that old crackhead we busted up with that two-by-four in the park. I bet he weren't no older than you, Mr. J."

Corelle always smiled when he was being ugly, knowing his ample charm could hang a jury as to the contents of his soul. The nastier the words, the bigger the smile. On this occasion he smiled so broadly that his eyes nearly closed—a trip and a hand up, a house fire and a bucket of water—perfectly ambiguous.

I gambled and called Corelle's bluff, choosing to trust the angel perched on one shoulder more than I feared the devil perched on the other. When Corelle asked the following day, I told him that he was indeed failing this quarter with a forty-eight, which was not surprising considering the fourteen assignments he had not completed. On that day my gamble was a good one. Rather than slashing my tires, Corelle inquired how he could possibly make up all the work he had missed, and if he did so would it still be possible to pass. Skeptical that he had the determination to complete it all, I assured him that he would pass if he finished all his incompletes in the next twenty-four hours. Corelle never stopped by that afternoon to pick up work or inquire about extra help, and I figured that his interest in my course had proven as fickle as his interest in the various girls who sat next to him in my classroom.

But the next morning, a few minutes after eight, Corelle and Marcus strolled into my room. They both had first-block classes that they were cutting, but that didn't seem to concern them: They had come about the makeup work. Still unconvinced, I opened the grade book and laid out for them what they were missing. I made a list that, by the time it was completed, included some fifteen grammar exercises, five to ten one-page journal entries, three five-paragraph essays, and a series of questions based on short stories we had read in class. The pair seemed undaunted and sat down to work.

The first period of the day was my conference period, so the three of us were left alone in the room for the first hour and a half. Because I was frantic with my own work, nearly an hour had passed before I realized that Corelle and Marcus had not spoken a word to each other, had not lifted their heads from their desks, and were steadily amassing a pile of work.

When the second-block bell rang, I was sure that they had reached their limit. A class full of rambunctious students would be entering their quiet haven, and the allure of the chaotic halls during class changes was too much for any self-respecting rabble-rouser to refuse. But Corelle and Marcus did not flinch, even as students entered the room and smaller, clumsier boys informed them that they had taken their seats. This did not break their focus, nor did it move them to let loose the onslaught of insults that would humiliate the awkward boys into finding a different desk to hide themselves under. The two moved expeditiously and resumed their work. Even the handful of attractive and flirtatious young women who were in my second block, of whom one was a once and future paramour of Corelle's, did not rouse them from their work. Amazingly, the second block passed like the first, interrupted occasionally with my recollection that they were present—heads still bent, pencils scribbling, paper stacks growing.

The ultimate test came later, when the thirty-seven inordinately loud students of my third block arrived. I thought that, among their own classmates, the situation would prove much too shameful for Marcus and Corelle, but again I underestimated them. At the first obvious sign of flirtation from one of his girls, Corelle made a loud announcement: "I can't be clowning up in here today, I be too busy trying to pass this mug before them good report cards come out tomorrow."

He commandeered the laughs himself, and people left him alone, surprisingly impressed although still entertained. While Marcus was not distracted by the class, his focus petered out early in third block, although not before he had completed most of the assignments.

It was after 2:00 when Corelle brought me his stack of work to turn in. For nearly six hours he had worked without a break, without a complaint, without a cigarette. In his stack were some thirty pages of material, all written in his same effusive hand, some of it poignant, much of it humorous, all of it thorough. Corelle passed that quarter with a seventy-two, and I could not decide whether I should change my system to prevent his pulling the same stunt four weeks later, or whether I would leave it exactly the same, if only to assure myself the chance of witnessing such a spectacle again.

For a while I was convinced that Corelle would be my first great victory. The most encouraging sign of this came just a few days after his makeup-work marathon in my room. Corelle arrived in my room with a particularly calm swagger one afternoon, still uninterested in schoolwork, but also ostensibly uninterested in the mayhem that went along with his appearance in class. Suddenly Corelle manifested the gap in age that had always existed between him and the rest of the students in my classroom. He kept primarily to himself that day, talking mostly with Marcus when he talked at all. At lunch he even came up to stand next to me at my nervous perch at the head of the table. Marcus soon drifted over next to us, as if the two were preparing to make a pitch.

"Well, Mr. J., we fittin' to bounce."

Uptight, I overreacted. "No way. Nobody leaves the lunchroom 'til we all finish and we go together."

"No. I ain't talking about no lunchroom. I'm talking about bouncing, like we out the building, we out of Greenville, we just out!"

"What are you talking about? Are you all moving or what?"

"Yeah, that's what I'm talking about, Mr. J. We moving up and out, we got us some tight jobs lined up working on dem race cars!"

I was confused. I knew Corelle worked after school at a body shop, but I couldn't see the connection between a one-man fix-it shop and the Indy 500.

After a lengthy conversation—the rest of the class let me know it had gone on too long when the roars from the table started escalating and the food started flying—I discovered that the science teacher, Mr. Thompson, a young white Southern man, had some connection through his father with an organization that staffed pit crews for the NASCAR circuit. Marcus and Corelle had Mr. Thompson for second block, and I considered it a testimony to my own failure that they both were docile in his room. Mr. Thompson had told me that, though they didn't necessarily complete assignments—and therefore would not pass the class—they sat quietly, and even participated on occasion. Mr. Thompson, like myself, had taken a special liking to this duo, and he too was troubled by their prospects.

What was frightening about Marcus and Corelle was the aggregate of latent strength and energy that shifted constantly across their broad shoulders. Their dangers were in fact nothing more than unrealized assets. Mr. Thompson hoped to harness that energy by getting them jobs working in one of the pit crews that his dad staffed. Both were able-bodied, both had experience working with cars; the rest could be taught. Both were nearly twenty, but neither had enough credits to be considered a sophomore in good standing. There was no visible movement toward graduation, and therefore nothing to keep them from hustling off to a job before the school year was over. Corelle and Marcus saw all these things too, and both jumped at the opportunity.

It soon became all the two talked about. Everyone in the class knew; most people in the school knew. Corelle had staked all his chips on this one chance. His misbehavior lessened considerably, as he no longer had to reconcile his academic failings with his hard-earned reputation as a clown. Instead he loafed like the arrogant senior who has already been admitted to his first-choice college. According to Corelle the job was all but secured. They were waiting to find out which race team the boys would be appointed to and when that team would be at a race nearby so the boys could rendezvous with them. There was little need to work, not because they were incapable, or had no interest, but because they had definitively moved beyond it.

In those weeks Corelle and I interacted more like friends than as teacher and student. He declined most invitations to do work the way one declines the offer of a cigarette, respectfully but without concern. As a result I did my best to provide things that might keep his interest: magazines, newspapers, poems, or current events that might help him on his way. We talked often of the details of his employment, and I could tell that he knew few. Where will you live? How long is the contract for? What does your mom say? He answered each question with that eager naïveté of the high school basketball player who has gone pro: jettisoned so quickly from dependence to independence, poverty to opulence, childhood to manhood, pupil to professional.

The weeks passed, but no news came from Mr. Thompson. Corelle no longer initiated conversations about the prospect and evaded questions. With the decline of those conversations, Corelle's new persona began to decay. His distance from his peers began to close once again. More girls talked to Corelle; more boys hovered around his chair seeking positions in his comical schemes.

It was on the day of our next test, some three weeks later, that Corelle first indicated his resignation to his former self. I had passed out the test and made the usual statement that no one was allowed to talk during the test and any infraction of this rule would result in my picking up their tests and assigning them a zero. The test had just landed on Corelle's desk when he scoffed at it and continued whispering sweet invitations to the girl next to him. He and I both knew that he was not asking for answers, both because he didn't care enough about them to seek them, and if he did, he possessed too much pride to procure them from an ingenue such as this. He wished only to test the rule in principle, perhaps to trap me into an argument where he could indignantly defend his own innocence for comic effect.

Though I knew that he was not cheating, I also knew that he was blatantly breaking the rule just to see what I would do about it. To ignore it meant to tacitly indicate that I would let students do whatever they wanted, while to enforce the rule was to incite an argument that might do more damage to the class than his trivial conversation ever could. I straddled the line for as long as I could, offering Corelle public and private warnings for the first five minutes of the test (something else I had said I would not do). Corelle cared nothing about the test, and thus had nothing to lose, but sought only to test me in the process.

Once the room had quieted, Corelle pushed the envelope, turning in a conspicuous whisper to his neighbor, "What's the answer to number six?"

"*Corelle,*" I warned once more.

Chuckles were spreading, noise was mounting, and Corelle pushed on: "Hey, I'll tell you right now that answer you just put down is wrong, any fool know that theme ain't where the story takes place."

The laughter erupted. Sensing order on the verge of eclipse, I had already reached Corelle's desk by the time his punch line landed. Before he could turn back to his desk I had whisked up his paper and started back toward the front of the room. The students' melodramatic "ooh's" urged Corelle to turn toward me when he noticed his empty desk. The fatal flaw in my plan was that once I had taken Corelle's test, he had even less to lose. I had given away the one bargaining chip I held.

Corelle stood up and began to yell full voice. "What you doing? You better give me back my test before I go buck-wild up in here. You about to see one nigga get 'bout it! I ain't playing now, I'm gonna tear this whole club up if you don't give me that test back! I wasn't gonna give that stupid ol' bald-headed girl the answer. She ain't none of mine no way!"

Corelle was standing on top of his desk, and my palliative gestures were becoming comical.

"Corelle, sit down. . . ."

"Corelle, if you want to talk about it we can. . . ."

"Corelle, I asked you three times not to talk. . . ."

"If you don't sit down, you're heading down to the office and then your chance is really gone."

His retorts were always more raucous, more sensible, and more popular than mine, and they only served to worsen the situation.

"My chance already be gone! What chance I got left? You done took my test, and now I got nothing to do but tear this room up 'til I GET MY TEST!"

Corelle stood so erect that his head brushed against the ceiling. He was directly opposite my desk and the filing cabinets, and once he spotted them he began hopping across the room from desk-top to desktop like a boy jumping from stone to stone to ford a river.

Mangling papers and upending backpacks as he went, the room was in full hysterics. He took one final leap from the end row toward my desk. He stepped behind my desk and flung open two drawers of the filing cabinet and turned to me.

"You better give me that test!"

Without waiting for a response, he pulled two handfuls of paper out of each cabinet and wielded them over his head like hand grenades without pins. For a moment I thought wearily of surrendering the test, but realized that the test was insignificant at this point.

Although I had already picked up a disciplinary referral form from my desk (I kept a stack of them nearby for third block), filling one out would be like threatening Al Capone with a traffic ticket. He dropped two stacks of the papers on top of the work table and they cascaded onto the floor. With two stacks still in hand, he turned to the bookshelves, where he picked three thick English books off the shelf.

"I want that test," he said. "Folks are fixing to get hurt!" His glance betrayed a wry smile that let me know his psychosis was affected, but also in his eyes was the assurance that his desire to affect it well was so pure that he was prepared to take any step toward insanity that the part required. The threat of flying books had sent girls diving under desks and boys jumping to their feet and picking up their own books, backpacks, and chairs in retaliation. It was Corelle's ride and I was only a passenger, strapped in until he decided the ride was over.

I could not bring myself to leave the room to call security, since his performance seemed to be hurtling too quickly toward climax—an explosion that would only be exacerbated by my absence. I managed to rescue a girl in the front row from under her desk and send her scuttling down the hall in search of security.

She had barely made it out the door when Corelle was inspired with a new idea. He dropped all the books with a triumphant crash, jumped up and over two desks—stepping on a girl's back and her backpack at the same time—and sprang toward the chalkboard. After slamming into the chalkboard, he snatched the jewel he was seeking: the fire extinguisher. He ripped the fire extinguisher from the wall, and with his hand on the nozzle, pointed it first at the class, threatening to take them hostage, then at me.

"Don't make me do it, Mr. J."

Now that the extinguisher was pointed at me, the students laughed and crept from their hiding places to watch Corelle's ebullient sunset. As I braced for the impact of thick gray dust, I noticed Corelle looking over my shoulder and lowering the fire extinguisher: Security had arrived.

I wrote Corelle up and sent him down to the office, only to see his face appear in my window twenty minutes later, solemn and betrayed. I went to the door, more curious than concerned. Corelle looked at me in disbelief.

"Man, you trying to get me suspended for a year or what? I didn't threaten you with no fire extinguisher."

Threatening a teacher was always a class-one offense, automatically mandating a hearing and generally a one-year expulsion or a one-year referral to alternative school. I had not considered this when I filled out the paper; I simply checked the box that read THREATENED A TEACHER. Despite his foolishness, I regretted the choice, if only for the vanquished look on Corelle's face. He was sad, not because he believed that he had gone too far, but because he thought I had misinterpreted how far he had actually gone. At that moment I wished that I could take back the check, but pragmatism and prudence dictated that it couldn't be done. I told Corelle that should he come to a hearing, I would be willing to testify against his removal from Greenville High, and then I watched him turn dejectedly and slide down the hall.

Perhaps Corelle just got tired of seriousness. Perhaps this was simply a show, and he a flawless actor wanting to parade a moment on the stage like the zealot who jumps the fence and sprints across the football field for a moment of unrivaled attention before he is apprehended and shuffled off to dire, lengthy consequences.

I believe that Corelle's antics erupted from the deep, dignified place inside him that understood with astonishing clarity what was right and wrong in his world. It was fitting that he chose to crucify himself on the cross of fairness. After years of numbing himself to the truth that hope was an illusion, he had—for a moment—boldly prepared himself to believe in the promise of opportunity. That promise had collapsed. And suddenly the notions of work and reward, desire and fulfillment, hope and happiness dangled like broken limbs—they were stories without strength, mass without meaning. For Corelle, fairness was how things were explained when they ended badly. Watching Corelle shuffle down the hall flanked by two security guards, a discomfort welled inside me.

Corelle's decline now accelerated precipitously. He came to class only to revel in his own ability to inspire laughter, discourage work, and pick up girls five years younger than he was. He was a masterful manipulator of his own image. He understood that after his hopes of moving on had been dashed, to return carefully to his old self would be to sneak in the back door of his own failure, to admit that he had gambled and lost. It was to return home ashamed and humbled by the world. If Corelle had to return to his old role of dissident and circus leader, he had to do it like all great performers—in the open, for everyone to see, and with great panache. In Greenville High School there is an unspoken awareness that communal time is dangerous time, precisely because it offers an open stage for anyone. If one is willing to trade a trip to the principal's office for a moment of fame (which most are), there is no riper time than a large gathering. As a result, larger gatherings and assemblies are avoided at all costs. The only sure place one can find an audience is at the school's communication hotline, the lunchroom.

Even though the staggered lunch periods spanned two and a half hours, should anything of significance happen there, the whole school would know long before the bell rang to end the third block. A thousand whispers would go forth in each passing in the hallways, while the teachers were picking up chalk or handing out an assignment. There was no greater testimony to the ability of an oppressed group to erect its own avenues of communication than the GHS underground. Corelle knew that, and he knew that the lunchroom was the communication nexus. He had been back in my class for only two days after his suspension following the fire extinguisher incident when he found another avenue for combustion.

Our assigned lunch table was in the farthest corner of the lunchroom, and as a result Corelle and Marcus always preferred to stand against the wall where they could see everyone, and where everyone could see them. Despite my constant urgings to sit down, they always managed to remain standing for a good portion of our lunch, partially because there were never enough chairs at our table to accommodate all thirty-seven of my students. I saw the genesis of the event quite clearly, and to their credit, Corelle and Marcus had nothing to do with it.

Our half of the lunchroom consisted of a row of rectangular tables, with two feet in between. The class next to us was also quite large, and it had one student who overflowed to a third table, with his back toward the rest of us. His classmates at the table adjacent to ours had begun throwing orange slices up into the air to see if they could catch them in their mouths. I had spotted this from the other end of the lunchroom and was heading over to stop it, already aware that their teacher was not going to do so. When I was within ten yards of the students, one of them let half an orange soar, arcing just slightly behind him. His aim was perfect; the half-orange landed directly on the tray of the solitary boy seated at the next table. I hurried in that direction, knowing that the situation had to be defused before it tumbled out of control.

The victim stood up and, as the perpetrator hoped, naturally assumed that the orange had come from my table. Without hesitation or question, he lifted his tray and the tray of a girl seated behind him, and with two sweeps of his arms emptied both trays in a long spray all over the eight students at the end of my table. Not coincidentally, since that was the end of the table where Corelle liked to stand, it was also where all the other would-be thugs in my class were concentrated. Two of them had taken the brunt of the spaghetti casserole bombardment and were justifiably incensed.

Though Corelle and Marcus were completely untouched, they seized the opportunity to use payback as a cover for inappropriate behavior. Both pounced on the trays lying on the table in front of them and slung them toward the aggressor. Corelle grabbed another tray and two whole oranges and threw them much farther across the lunchroom, hoping to incite the rest of the cafeteria to join. I was watching the trajectory of Corelle's toss when I spotted an orange coming straight at me. I stepped aside quickly enough that it only hit me on the leg, though it exploded all over my pants and left a noticeable sting for the rest of the afternoon. Fortunately, security arrived just as Corelle and some others had run out of trays and were preparing to throw fists.

This time the ax fell swiftly and definitively on Corelle and Marcus. Although there were some nine or ten boys involved in the fray, Corelle's conspicuousness worked against him. The security guards had seen him standing against the wall; they knew his face and his record and were delighted at the chance to book him for something that might lead to an ultimate expulsion. There were six days left until our third term exams and Thanksgiving break. Corelle and Marcus were given three days' suspension and three days in PAC, a disciplinary program that isolated misbehaving students in a separate room but allowed them to complete class assignments. The days of regular suspension were unexcused absences and could not be made up. During their days in PAC, should the boys come in, they would be eligible to take any tests given. I doubted that I would see Corelle again before Thanksgiving, but I did not expect that I would never see him at Greenville High School again.

It was nearly a month later, three days before Christmas vacation, that I received the following notice in my mailbox: "Please drop the following students from your rolls, they is no longer enrolled in Greenville High School."

There were perhaps thirty students' names on the list. There was Damien, who was in my homeroom, and who had told me that he came to school only for the free meal, and because none of his "clients" wanted to get high before lunch. And, Simone, who had been in my English II class until she left to deliver her second child. Then, skimming to the bottom of the page, my heart skipped a beat: Corelle Wright.

SEVEN

Larry was the third block's other pillar of chaos, seated at the opposite corner of the room from Corelle. When Corelle was industrious or absent, Larry carried the burden of disruption. He shared Corelle's ability to make me feel small. He was only slightly taller than I was but without being obese, he had a girth that gave him a seventy-five-pound advantage. Although there is seldom a situation in which a teacher feels he may come to blows with a student, a first-year male teacher struggling to establish authority has a palpable disadvantage with students who know that they are physically superior. Like villagers living in the shadow of a slumbering volcano, you must always watch for signs.

It was after he failed his first test that Larry's rebellion began. His first step was to stop doing work altogether. From the beginning of class to the end of class he did not pick up a pencil or crack a book unless it was to damage it. In a smaller class, or a better managed one, I might have developed a method to address Larry's noncompliance, but since I was constantly struggling to maintain enough quiet for those few students who were trying to work effectively, I had neither the time nor the wherewithal to address Larry.

If it is ever true that idle hands find evil work, it is true in a classroom. Larry's first project was to rip the wooden laminate off the desk where he sat in the farthest corner of the room. He went about it like a prisoner burrowing in the dead of night. With nearly two and a half vacant hours at that desk each day, none of which was used to do work, he had plenty of time. It took him a few days to loosen the wood from the body of the desk, and once he had successfully loosened one corner he began work on the other. This complete, he began delaminating the wood from both corners of the desk. The desk soon looked as dog-eared as an old driver's license. Like many of the other disruptions in the third block, I had been monitoring Larry's progress on the desk, but had never caught him in the act. Because two other students sat at his desk during other periods, to accuse him without firsthand evidence could start a disruption more violent than I cared to venture into.

Larry was far more dangerous and enigmatic than Corelle. He had learned to live life physically. I had heard him tell stories about his father's beatings with a mixture of pride and venom. When he was in one of his rages, nothing I could say made any difference to Larry. With a different student I might have put a hand on his shoulder and guided him to his seat, but Larry's rage promised that he would not tolerate my coming anywhere near him.

The first incident occurred with a scrawny girl who sat in the middle of the room. Shakena was mercilessly ridiculed for being cross-eyed. As a result she had grown up with more than a sizable chip on her shoulder. She had learned that the only way to stop persecution, or to refute it, was to fight. I saw her pick fights with the three largest boys in my room before she was eventually removed from my class. She would begin with a glare, proceed to a slap or a scratch, and often end in a wild assault of flailing arms, fingernails, and feet. Because Larry was always looking for some form of entertainment to make his idle time in my classroom pass more quickly, his attention often lighted on Shakena. In addition to her pugilistic eagerness, Shakena had also developed an ability to zero in on a student's greatest insecurity and bare it for all to see. It was a well-tested method of self-defense. Early in the year she discovered Larry's Achilles' heel: his academic record. Larry had been held back two years in middle school. After spending a year in the alternative school for threatening to kill a teacher, he was promoted to the ninth grade without ever passing the eighth. Shakena, like many of the other students, knew this, and was quick to mention it any time Larry made comments about her.

I was helping someone in the front of the room, and by the time I noticed the disruption—a disruption louder than the continuous mayhem—Shakena was on her feet and Larry was walking toward the front of the room. That was when Larry's pacing began. No one rose to detain Larry, since everyone knew it would do little more than get someone hurt or humiliated. Larry harbored a profound disinterest in any of the disciplinary methods available to me: He would not serve detention, the office did not frighten him, and days at home would only be better than days in school. He had already experienced the most severe punishment the school district had to offer—the alternative school—and it was no longer a threat. He knew he was failing my class and it was clear he didn't respect me as a teacher or a human being; therefore, I held absolutely no authority over him. He continued pacing, talking more to himself than anyone else. Never had I seen more clearly the process of one's id and superego vying for supremacy. His id had taken control of his entire body, and it shook and writhed, longing to be satisfied. But from somewhere within, the smallest voice—one of the few in the world that Larry probably still heard—was telling him that this was not the time to deal with Shakena.

I assigned Larry Saturday detention for his outburst. Fortunately he realized that it would be bad form to pummel a scrawny little girl in the middle of English class, so eventually he paced his way back to his seat. He skipped the Saturday detention, like all the others he had skipped. When the school's paperwork caught up with him he would have to serve the detention, but he and I both knew that the paperwork moved slowly. He also knew that even when it moved, there were ways around it. As a result, I decided it was time to do two things: start my own detention for my students from the third block, and call Larry's mother. I told Larry that he would have detention the following day after school in my room. He laughed and disregarded it, telling me that he had heard that before and he still wasn't going.

That night I called Larry's mother, and we had a rather agreeable conversation. I told her Larry was failing because he refused to do the work, and that he continued to be a discipline problem and a disruption. She told me she was one of the cooks at Morrison's cafeteria, and gave me her work number there, should I ever have more problems with Larry. She promised me he would be at detention the following day, Tuesday, and that he would walk home. I was encouraged by that conversation, so much so that the next day I almost didn't notice Larry laboring over one of the grammar exercises in the back of the room.

Late that afternoon I was sitting motionless after the final bell, trying to recover from another day the way a soldier does, recounting the horrors, clinging to the few fond memories, and counting it a success because I had survived to count it at all. I was trying to quiet my beating heart, pick up papers, and straighten books when Larry showed up at my door for detention.

I had made a plan for Larry's visit. The night before, I had packed my chessboard in my schoolbag. Chess was a pedagogical tool that I had decided upon the previous summer, when my thoughts about school were wistful and lucid, rather than overbearing and futile in the way they had become recently. Although I had not played chess since I was little, it occurred to me that it would be a perfect, and perhaps entertaining, teaching tool. Larry would be my test case.

He asked where he should sit, anticipating the perfunctory hour of placing his head on his desk that he was familiar with from the school's regular detention policy. Instead I guided him over to the table next to my desk and offered him the seat across from me. While he settled in I crossed to the oversized dictionary sitting on top of the filing cabinet. Along with the four walls and the desks, it was the one thing I had inherited along with this room, simply because no one ever wanted to move it. It must have weighed forty pounds and was eight inches thick. The spine had disappeared and it had become a stack of loose yellowed papers with faded minuscule black print. I flipped through until I found the definition for "integrity," and wrote the word along with the definition on the board. Larry glanced at it quizzically. I sat down and took my chessboard out of my bag.

"I'm going to teach you a game," I said, "that will hopefully be more interesting and more instructive than simply sitting here for an hour."

It was my favorite of all the boards that I had seen, wooden, folded in half with small magnets that held the two ends together and held all the pieces inside. On top where it closed, a small wooden hole had been carved out, so you could carry it like a briefcase.

"Chess. Have you ever played chess before?"

He shook his head.

"Okay," I said, "well, I'm going to teach you. That way when you go home today and your mom asks you what you learned at school today, instead of saying 'Nothing,' you can say, 'Actually, Mom, I learned how to play chess.'"

I emptied the pieces out onto the table and unfolded the board. I took the brown pieces and began lining them up in front of me. When playing against my students, I frequently played with the brown pieces to prevent the color of the pieces and the color of the players from meaning more than they should.

I began by teaching Larry how to set up the pieces, and then started teaching him how the pieces moved. Once he had learned the basics we started a game, knowing that the lessons would be the most clear once he had already seen them for himself. Larry was reticent to the point that I thought I would have to force him to move his first piece or that he might throw the whole board off the table and refuse to play. I had thrown him in without much introduction to the game, and Larry demonstrated a mild degree of learned helplessness—so used to being wrong when he chose one thing, wrong when he chose the other, wrong when he did not choose at all.

Eventually he loosened up, perhaps emboldened by the sense that each move was equally futile. It was quickly evident that Larry was not a fast learner: He had a hard time recognizing when his pieces were in danger of being taken, and was not very creative about finding solutions once he recognized danger. He brooded long and hard over each move. Nor was he perceptive about pieces of mine that I had left openly vulnerable to capture. He seemed afraid that capturing them might incur some greater and unseen punishment.

Nonetheless, we continued. I probed delicately but consistently, hoping that he would follow my model and attempt some risks of his own. He never generated much offense. He moved pieces in a haphazard and perfunctory manner when he was not in immediate danger, withdrawing when he was. Prepared to add pressure, I moved my bishop into an undefended position where I could capture his queen. However, he could also use his queen to capture my bishop without putting her in any jeopardy. He studied both the pieces after I moved, looking hard at them, his cumbersome fingers levitating over the board like a wrecking ball, his bulky hands paralyzed in indecision. After a long moment he disregarded those two pieces and switched his focus to the other side of the board, deliberating between moving two equally insignificant pawns. He chose one of the pawns and moved it one space forward, then looked up at me to see if he had answered incorrectly.

I could see that he felt a bit stranded, and that with his queen in jeopardy it was a good moment to impart some wisdom.

"There are a few golden rules to chess," I said. "The first is that you cannot survive without a plan, and in order to have a plan you must always think three steps ahead of where you are. You have to start by making a plan for what you want to accomplish, and when you have decided that, then you have to stop to think about what sequence of small steps you must take in order to accomplish that. Then you must always watch three or four moves ahead in order to make sure that the plan is going as you intended. Ask yourself, 'Where do I want to be five steps down the road, and what am I going to do to make sure I get there?' That's the first rule, make a plan, and map out each small step you must take to get there.

"The second rule has to do with protecting yourself as you try to reach that goal. The second rule is this: Every action has a consequence, even if you don't see those consequences right away. As a result, before you make any move you have to stop and think to yourself, 'What might happen if I do this? What good might happen and what bad might happen?' Then you evaluate each possible part of the decision. If in your evaluation you discover that more bad may come from that move than good, it is probably not a good move. What you can't do is be careless. That's how you get killed. When you just start moving for no reason, just moving because you've got nothing better to do, you can be sure somebody else is going to take advantage of your mistakes and use them to his own advantage."

I gestured toward the word that I had written on the board. "Now there's one more thing, and this is just my own way of looking at this game. Do you know this word behind me?"

He shook his head.

I read aloud what I had written on the board: "Integrity:

soundness of moral character, wholeness or completeness." It read with the clumsiness of a poem translated through three languages, an extremely diluted but recognizable version of the original. I pointed to the brown king. "This is your life. You lose him, the game's over. The way I see this game, there are things more important than just staying alive." I raised the brown queen triumphantly. "This is your integrity. Without integrity, life is almost worthless. You may be able to creep along with a pulse and a full stomach, patiently waiting for your life to be taken, but without integrity you've lost the wholeness, you're a walking shadow. In everything you do on this board, in every move you make, every decision you consider, your first commitment always has to be to protect your integrity. Even if there are great gains to be made, but they mean sacrificing integrity, the gains can't be worth it, for nothing is worth more than your integrity—not even your life. Even if you lose you can always look back at the game and be proud if you kept your integrity; you can be proud, not because of what you've done but because of how you've done it. That's the object of this game, to play with dignity and principle. That's the object of every game."

I stopped, realizing I had probably gone too far. But when I refocused on Larry's face I knew immediately that he had not missed a word. That my metaphor was not faithful to the sophisticated chess strategy made no difference. His big hands were finally resting, and the largeness of his face was at ease with a graceful focus that I had not seen before. He had arrived in my room for the first time, and he was waiting for more.

"That is why I taught you this game instead of having you sit here with your head down for an hour. I don't care about you wasting an hour of your life to make up for acting like a fool in class. I don't want *revenge* for you disrupting my class; I want to help you understand that every move you make without thinking puts you deeper in trouble, just like chess. If you just keep drifting through each day not thinking about tomorrow, you're going to get eaten up. A chessboard has only thirty-two pieces on it, sixteen pieces for you and sixteen against you, and already you can see how tricky it is, how easy it is to get careless and make a stupid choice that costs you a bishop or even a queen. Greenville has forty-five thousand people in it, and you can't just look at the colors and figure out who's for you and who's against you. That means it's that much more complicated, it's that much easier to get careless and make a stupid choice.

"When you do things like getting thrown out of class every day, getting into fights, failing classes, you're making bad choices, you're not thinking about the consequences. If you clown around today, you miss the lesson, then you miss the assignment, then when the test comes around, you've never seen the stuff before, and you probably fail it. That cycle repeats itself until the next thing you know you're left like your friend Anthony, twenty years old and still in the tenth grade with nowhere to go. You're there because you weren't thinking about how every action has a consequence."

I pressed this example to reach some of my deeper concerns about Larry's involvement with some boys who had been scuffling with a local gang called OMP, short for the Ohio-Mulberry Posse. "You go out cruising with your friends from Eighth Street on Friday night, just because some of them are your boys, not thinking about what the consequences might be. Then when you roll by a few of those fellas from OMP, you find out one of your boys has a gun, and he decides he might just unload a few shots on OMP for that nonsense they were talking at Hollywood Palace last week. Next thing you know they're shooting back, and bullets are busting through the window and tearing up the wall behind your head, all because three moves back, you didn't stop to see what the consequences might be. Now all of a sudden it might cost you your life. Worse still, you might be packing yourself, or you might grab the .357 that Crack always keeps under the seat and you start firing back in a moment of panic. You might hit one of those boys in the other car—you might. But more likely you hit the six-year-old girl riding her tricycle in the front yard next door. Now you've done worse than give up your life, you've given up the only really valuable thing you ever had to lose: your integrity. You've stopped playing the game with moral character.

"In this little board game today, I was playing *against* you. Sometimes you think that in this classroom I'm playing against you too, but I'm not. I'm playing with you. The reason I stay on you is because I damn sure don't want to see you walk into a bullet. With the boys you're rolling with and the attitude you're taking, right now you're making choices you're not thinking about. Choices with consequences." I slid the bishop diagonally across the board, motioning to take his queen, and then retreated my bishop to where it was.

Larry's eyes did not leave me for a long time, until he slowly lowered his head back to the board, and surveyed his side. Without his queen I could see that his random gathering of pieces looked every bit as porous as they were. He watched the chessboard but showed no interest in moving his pieces.

For a number of minutes Larry was quiet. Not just quiet, but pensive. Ignorant of the weight of the silence, his eyes bored holes through the table.

A voice boomed down the hall, "Anybody in here? We're locking up."

I looked at my watch: It was after five. Larry and I had been at it for more than an hour and a half. We both realized we needed to go, but neither was willing to acknowledge that the threat of being locked in the building was more important than closure to this conversation.

"You played a good game, Larry, and there's still a whole lot left of the game that counts. This one's just for practice. And I wouldn't have brought you here if I didn't think you could win. . . ."

I realized that I would not be able to close the door on the conversation, because he was still holding the door open, but I did not know why, and so I tried to lighten the heaviness. "You've got to get going so your mom doesn't get worried about you. I don't think there's enough floor space for two of us to sleep in here."

Larry lumbered to his feet and started toward the door, his head still fixed on the floor. I feared that perhaps I had gone too hard on him, the weight of penitence evident not just in his eyes but in his slumped shoulders and the shuffle of his feet.

"Larry," I said, "do you have a ride home?"

He turned back toward me but could not look up. "Yes, sir. I'll be all right." He raised his powerful hand and weakly waved good-bye, then shuffled out the door.

I had heard Larry call me "Mike" and "punk" and "weak" and "cracker" and "dumbass" and even "fucker" under his breath. Usually, when he wanted something he just said "Hey," refusing to offer the perfunctory respect that would accompany the title "Mr." I never imagined that he would call me "sir." I fell back into my chair and stayed there until I was jarred by the rattling of the chains across the door downstairs.

When I drove out of the parking lot and started home, I saw Larry walking north toward his house in patient strides—eyes fixed straight ahead. I knew he didn't have a ride when I asked him back in the classroom, but that was the way he wanted it.

EIGHT

Two months after school began a new student entered my second-block class. When he first appeared at my door in the middle of my second block, I suspected that he was a troublemaker looking for a good prank. As he continued knocking on the door I could no longer ignore him. Months of being fooled by tricksters had taught me to demand a copy of his schedule before I let him cross my room's threshold. Much to my surprise, he pulled a crumpled schedule from his pocket. I scanned the page for my name: "English II: Johnston, 227. Jevon Jenkins." He stood barely six feet tall, but was the heaviest student I had seen on campus. Jevon was dark-skinned but his face was splotched with patches of brighter skin, as if he'd been severely burned. His arms were covered from wrist to biceps with tattoos; two I recognized as familiar gang emblems, the Deuces and CCP—the Carver Circle Posse. His vacant stare implied that he was incapable of humor or affection, cold enough that a visible show of disinterest might take some serious conjuring.

He did not seem to know anyone in the classroom, and after I approved his schedule he walked to the opposite corner of the room without instruction. He sat in one of the three wide rectangular desks I had placed along the back wall. He was too large to fit in one of the regular desks. Emmanuel, one of the student band directors, had already taken the large desk on the other side of the room, so I couldn't contest Jevon's seat choice. My biggest trouble with Emmanuel was that I would often find him at his desk composing classical music rather than working on the current assignment.

Jevon carried no accessories whatsoever—no backpack, jacket, pen, notebook; nothing. Sadly, this was rather common at Greenville High School; it was in part a protest because locker privileges had been revoked two years earlier due to security concerns. Students had to transport all their belongings and all their books, and setting them down even for a minute meant exposure to theft or vandalism. For some students, their refusal to acquire school supplies articulated their attitudes toward school in general: They would agree to show up each day as the law and their parents mandated, and they would sometimes agree not to keep others from learning, but this did not mean they had to expend their own time and energy to help the process run more smoothly. I guessed that even Jevon's pockets were empty, except for perhaps a lighter and a crumpled up cigarette.

Jevon acted much like the rest of the students on their first day: passive, restrained, calculating. After his comfort level grew, he made casual acquaintance with a few of the marginal characters who occupied the back of the room. One of them, Bryant, who generally was in school only two days a week, had taken a liking to Jevon, mostly due to a common interest in obtaining cigarettes and drug paraphernalia during the day. Toward the end of his second week, Jevon asked to go to the bathroom, saying his stomach hurt horribly and he had been sick all morning. Since this was his first request, I granted it. Naturally I continued the class, but some thirty minutes later I noticed that Jevon's desk was still empty. As the rest of the class was making sporadic efforts at some independent work, I ventured out into the hallway to search for Jevon. Much to my surprise, when I stepped into the hallway he was but a few feet away.

"Where have you been for the last thirty minutes?"

"I've been in the bathroom. Sick. I don't feel so good." He looked at the floor, deferential but not penitent. He was lying and he didn't care that I knew.

Perhaps he was curious to see how I'd handle an obvious lie that I could not prove. He still looked at the ground and shifted his feet like a boy. I looked at his tattoos; there was one on each forearm that I could not decipher, each set off by long scars that ran down his arms. In this moment when he was caught, his idiosyncrasies were still boyish, but I could feel them evolving into more worrisome habits. I chose to handle the situation by straddling a line of discipline, assuring him he couldn't expect bathroom privileges in the future. He nodded indifferently and passed back into the room. In the back of the room his surly partner, Bryant, looked up, and as he did I saw a wide smile spread across Jevon's face— the first I had ever seen. I realized then that I had erred on the side of leniency, and the effect would become obvious.

Jevon soon missed three days while the class was at work on group projects, and he returned on the day before the project's culmination. I had almost forgotten about him when the tardy bell rang for second block. As the crowd cleared, dispersing with haste into their various rooms, a solitary figure was revealed lumbering down the hall. Jevon was late, had missed a number of days, and was about to miss the test grade that the next day's projects represented.

When he reached the doorway, I told him that he had fallen behind on an assignment that was due the following day, and that he needed to work hard that day in order to receive a passing grade. He looked straight through me. Whatever he had seen in the three days of his absence, its intensity had made human figures inconsequential. I handed him a copy of the presentation topics and told him to get started right away. Without looking at it, he collected it the way a truck collects an insect on its windshield. He did not greet the small cadre of boys with whom he had grown familiar, nor did he acknowledge the rest of his class-mates. Slightly disturbed by his manner, I watched him all the way to his seat. Noticing my attention, the students grew anxious them-selves. I chose to disregard Jevon, and to do my best to proceed with the business of class.

Once I had gotten the students started on their work, I re-turned my attention to Jevon. Though I hadn't studied him closely during my instructions, I did notice that he was working on some-thing, and I was moderately pleased. Perhaps his new disposition was in fact a wake-up call to the urgency of his own situation.

But as I started back toward Jevon's desk, I soon saw the fruits of his labor: On his desk he had spread out hundreds of shreds from the paper I had handed him. I told him that he must clean up the shredded paper and obtain a copy of the assignment from some-one else before the class was over. He looked up and, with his eyes trained on me, swept the shreds off his desk and watched them sprinkle to the ground. Then he propped his big elbow on the desk and extended his pudgy middle finger directly at me.

I sent him to the principal's office.

The next occurrence was less than two weeks later. I was down in the annex during my conference period when I noticed Mr. Taylor, the history teacher, marching his class out into the open field behind the annex. I saw Jevon in the back of the group. Some-how Jevon noticed me up in the second-floor window, and when Mr. Taylor looked the other way, Jevon held his giant arm aloft and once again shot me the middle finger. Not wanting to engage in a disciplinary struggle with a student in someone else's class, I walked away from the window and thought for a minute. While running errands, I found myself in the downstairs annex ten min-utes later when Mr. Taylor's class came filing in from the field. Jevon was again at the end of the line. Knowing he was coming I waited outside the door to see if he would acknowledge his earlier gesture. He swaggered toward me, smiling. He stared at me with a wry grin and then suddenly threw both of his hands toward me in a defiant gesture that mimicked rap stars.

"What you gonna do, huh?" he sneered. "What you gonna do?"

He continued staring at me as he passed close enough to threaten a punch, and certainly close enough to deliver one. Then he curled his hand into a gun, pointed it at the lockers and fired, releasing a guttural boom as his arm kicked back from the explosion. He turned toward me as he continued walking, holding his phony smoking gun aloft as he watched imaginary gunpowder swirl off the barrel.

As he reached the end of the hallway, he pointed his makeshift gun directly at me and said, "See that! That's what happens if I fail!"

He turned away and with a wide enticing smile he let his pudgy brown hand relax. I looked at my watch; in twenty-two minutes Jevon would be arriving in my room for second block.

I decided to turn to Mr. Hudson, the assistant principal, for advice. Mr. Hudson and Mr. Amos together made up the entire administration of Greenville High School. Mr. Hudson spent the entire day dealing with discipline. Every time a teacher "wrote up" a student—filled out a disciplinary referral form—the student was sent to Mr. Hudson's office. Mr. Hudson hollered at kids when they needed to be hollered at, and told them to shut their traps when they needed to shut them. The only complaint I ever heard about Mr. Hudson was that he too readily believed in the inherent goodness of the students he disciplined. He was blessed with the patience of a father and the devotion of a preacher.

There was a similarity between the entrance to Mr. Hudson's office and the local street corner on a Friday night: Both were bustling with riffraff waiting for something to happen. For repeat offenders this area became a reliable and often enjoyable hangout spot, a perch from which they could heckle any passersby, knowing they were already in trouble. For predominantly good kids who took pride in their reputation as decent students, being spotted on the wall outside Mr. Hudson's office was Greenville High's version of the Puritan stocks, an obvious social stigma. On this particular morning, business was a bit quieter than usual, since the penitent outnumbered the proud.

Like a seasoned FBI agent, Mr. Hudson responded to my mention of Jevon Jenkins with the wistful frustration over the one that kept getting away.

"Yeah, we've been tracking him now for some time. What we got to do is get enough of a paper trail on him that we can take him to a hearing."

The hearing was the school district's highest court. It was a small and sundry court, presided over by the school board, where the defendant was present and the plaintiff—the school's representative (usually Mr. Hudson) or a slighted teacher—brought forth testimony and witnesses to bear upon the defendant's guilt. This elaborate legal process was necessary because the school board could hand out the severest form of disciplinary punishment—it could either dismiss students or refer them to alternative settings, in our case Garrett Hall, the alternative school.

Mr. Hudson raised his head from his papers to give me my assignment: "Document everything you got. Each event on a separate referral form, and bring them all to me, and we'll get this started. For now we'll see if we can get you a parent conference. Ms. Coris has been having some trouble with him too."

I returned to my room and began to write up the events, waiting for the toll of the bell. I had just begun the second referral when the bell rang and the first of my second-block students filtered through the door. Mr. Taylor's class was only two doors down from mine, so Jevon was always one of the first to arrive. I did not go to the doorway to look for him. Instead, I stayed in the room and conversed with the two students who had already arrived. A moment later Jevon arrived without salutation and proceeded disinterestedly to his place in the corner. We were a good deal of the way through class before I heard from Jevon again. As before, he had been occupied with some labor at his desk. I didn't suspect that it was the assignment the rest of the class was working on, but he seemed to be doing some writing of his own kind: harmless enough. He raised his hand to call me back to his desk.

He had a blank notebook sitting squarely on his desk and I wondered what had happened to the fruits of his labor. He asked plainly if he could go to the bathroom. Without pleading he told me that he would not take long and I could watch him from the doorway if I liked. The boys' bathroom was in direct sight of my doorway. With my monitoring, his trip could not last long enough to commit either of the most common bathroom offenses: gambling and smoking. I conceded, more out of curiosity than courtesy, anxious to see if he was trying to get himself into trouble or steer clear of it. I granted his request and returned to the front of the room. As I did so, out of the corner of my eye I caught Jevon flashing a toothy smile at his partner, Bryant. I watched Jevon raise his considerable body from his desk and stand in front of Bryant, and watched Bryant reach into his backpack and pull something out, placing it furtively in Jevon's hands. Bryant smiled sheepishly at me and quickly returned his eyes to his blank paper. Jevon also put his head down and moved slowly but steadily towards the door.

I stepped in front of the door. "You need to give me whatever's in that hand."

"What? There ain't nothing."

"Give it to me, Jevon, or you go back to your seat."

By now Jevon and I had taken center stage; the entire class looked up from their papers to see how this would be resolved. Jevon no longer wished to deny that there was something in his hand; he simply refused to turn it over. I looked at the thickness of his hand and I knew that any attempt to force it from him would be futile, but I refused to let him out of my supervision with it.

"I'm just going to the bathroom. Just let me go to the bathroom, you already said I could." His eyes did not once raise to meet mine.

"It comes to me or you go to your seat, Jevon. It's that simple."

He thought for a minute, shuffling one foot and raising his head a little to look back toward the class. I moved slightly from the doorway, in part because I believed he had made his decision to return to his seat, and in part because I feared he was on the verge of snapping and barging out the door. He turned without comment or ceremony and returned to his desk. The class shifted in their seats and mumbled a few comments. Some minutes later I was leaning over a student's desk proofreading an essay when I heard a chair squeak. I raised my eyes to see Jevon, backpack in hand, rising from his desk and walking, without urgency, toward the door. He made no show of defiance or disrespect, but simply chose to leave. I knew that to call to him with any urgency would only weaken my already debilitated position.

He had made up his mind, and that decision included disregarding consequences. I knew it would be worthless to threaten him with them now.

"I'll see you in the office, Jevon," I called after him. Disconcerted, I looked back over to his desk. A muffled laughter erupted from the two boys who sat closest to Jevon. I walked over to get a better look.

In the middle of the desk, in permanent black marker, Jevon had drawn an incredibly graphic picture of a man and woman having sex. The drawing itself was about the size of a notebook pad, and it was placed so perfectly in the center of the desk that it seemed almost like a place mat awaiting future visitors. I sent all my referrals to Mr. Hudson that afternoon, including the new one, and three days later I had a parent conference scheduled with Jevon's mother.

I had forgotten about the conference, and was busy preparing for my second block, when Jevon's mother poked her head in my doorway.

"Hello, are you Mr. Johnston?"

A bit surprised, I told her I was.

"I am Jevon Jenkins's mother. I'm here for a conference." Julie Coris, Jevon's French teacher, entered the room right behind her. The three of us sat down, Jevon's mother and I obviously unfamiliar with what should happen next.

Julie started by telling Jevon's mother that the source of his problems in her class were not his fault. Jevon had been placed in her French II class, though he had never taken French I. Julie told her that she had gone to the counselor several times to request a schedule change. However, the counselors said that since Jevon had arrived a month and a half late, all other classes were full and they wanted to leave him there and "see how he does." Julie concluded with a clear prognosis: "There is no way Jevon will pass."

"Yes," Jevon's mother said, "that's what I'm wondering, is does he have any chance to pass at all? If he starts doing all his work and he gets some makeup work?"

My fantasy of Jevon completing makeup work was snuffed by Julie's abrupt response: "No, there is just no way."

His mother then turned to make me the same offer; I glanced through the grade book at the string of zeros and naked boxes where grades were meant to be, wincing like a salesman offered a low price. For a moment I thought of Corelle's heroic makeup efforts.

"He seems capable of doing the work, that doesn't seem to be the problem. But he's very far behind in many of the basic skills, and I am not sure he would be able to catch up with the rest of the kids," I told her. I watched her eyes, and I glanced back toward Jevon's cave in the back of the room. I imagined him as a student rather than a menace, and I couldn't let this offer slip away. "But as far as the numbers go, if he worked hard for the rest of the year, and made up all the assignments that he has missed . . . yes, he could still pass."

She was visually pleased and sensed that it was her turn to speak.

"Well, see, this has all gone back so far, but when we finally brought him to Greenville High they had told me that he was all on grade level, but then he got in trouble so fast that we had to send him back to that military school again, and so we've never even gotten to figure out where he's really at."

Julie and I sensed that we had happened upon a clue to the riddle we had both been studying for weeks, and we pressed her to tell us Jevon's story from the beginning. It was so unbelievable, and so obvious, that I scratched down notes as quickly as I could, hoping to find some ledge in the wall of Jevon's past, a place where he and I could perhaps find a foothold and begin to climb again. By the time the story was over, I could see all the little places along the way where she had lost the small but invaluable battles, and the moment when she finally gave up, handing her boy over to God, unaware that often it is not God who comes first to claim those who have been left to him.

She said that Jevon was born in Jackson and spent his first three years of school there. He presented such discipline problems in the second grade that she and his teachers decided to send him to an "alternative school" for a year. I had never heard of a third grader being sent to alternative school, but if it resembled the alternative schools at the high school level then it must have been an eye-opening experience for a seven-year-old. As most teachers will acknowledge, a good portion of disciplinary problems arises from the defense mechanisms of students who feel insecure about their ability to do the work. Even Jevon's mother acknowledged that the situation was no different for Jevon; part of his problem, she said, stemmed from the fact that he wasn't as "quick" as the rest of the kids. After the year at the alternative school, Jevon was returned to fourth grade at his old school. If Jevon had not left for alternative school, he would have been retained in the second grade, based on his academic ability. Instead, he was sent to the alternative school for disciplinary reasons and after one year returned as a fourth grader.

This kind of mistake is notorious in public schools. In the Delta it has grown so common that many families use it as a strategy for promotion: If a child is failing a grade, send him to stay with an aunt in a neighboring county, where he will be enrolled in a grade based on his age. After a few months, return that child to the old school system where he will again be placed in a grade level according to his age, thereby executing a promotion without any work.

Jevon continued to exhibit the same behavior when he returned to the public elementary school in Jackson, so before Christmas he was sent back to the alternative school for another year. He returned a year later and was admitted to the fifth grade. As is common, the alternative school had made some inroads at curtailing his insolence, but had not seriously addressed his academic deficiencies; as a result, Jevon failed the fifth grade two years in a row. Since Jevon was then thirteen years old and already weighed more than two hundred pounds, the principal thought it emotionally unhealthy to retain Jevon for another year in the elementary school. The principal was at a loss: He couldn't in good faith promote a student who did not have the necessary skills, but neither could he retain a student who was so socially and emotionally removed from his peers that interaction was likely to be unhealthy for both parties. The answer with Jevon always seemed to be, "Send him to someone else." With some assistance from the principal, Jevon's mother decided to send him to Boys' Town in Memphis, a much larger, better resourced, privately run school for troubled boys. He spent two years at Boys' Town. Convinced that Jevon had made some progress, his mother and he moved to Greenville. Now fifteen years old, with his last formal school experience having been in the fifth grade, Jevon enrolled as a freshman at Greenville High School.

To no one's surprise, Jevon was well behind his classmates academically, and was socially uncomfortable because he had not been in a normal school environment since the fifth grade. He was unsuccessful in two tries at that level. Also to no one's surprise, his anxiety manifested itself in a continual display of discipline problems. Before he had the chance to illustrate that he was failing due to inadequate academic preparation, Jevon was removed from Greenville High School before Thanksgiving for fighting, and placed in Garrett Hall. The alternative school obtained a record of Jevon's past, and informed him that if he could successfully complete what it outlined as the skill requirements for sixth, seventh, and eighth grades during the eight months that he was there, he could return to the ninth grade.

Apparently Jevon worked diligently over those months, and he was reinstated to the ninth grade at Greenville High School the following year. But again his disciplinary problems persisted, and his academic preparation was inadequate; again he was removed before the semester was over. This time he was sent to the Dogwood School. The Dogwood School was both more militaristic and more evangelical than any of the others, believing that enough exposure to regimentation and to the Bible could cure anyone. Unfortunately, Dogwood ran on a different schedule from Greenville High, so it was not until October that he was released from Dogwood and enrolled in Greenville High School as a tenth grader.

This is why Jevon arrived two months late to English II, French II, world history, and algebra II. He was expected to outrace his peers to compensate for the missed lessons, although the last time he had successfully passed a course in school was ten years earlier, in the second grade. Counselors placed him in French II and English II, despite the fact that he had never taken—never mind passed— English I or French I. As his mother finished her story I sat enraged, wanting to burn public education to the ground and start again just for Jevon. I glanced over her shoulder at the calendar: It was almost Thanksgiving, and Jevon was right on schedule.

To his credit, Jevon lasted until Christmas. He failed my class with a sixty, despite some marked improvements. One day the following semester, I picked up the newspaper as I waited for a faculty meeting to begin, and recognized Jevon's photograph on the front page. I wanted not to read it, already knowing what it would say. Jevon had been arrested and convicted of three different offenses. Two instances of armed robbery did not surprise me; it was the third that broke my heart. Jevon had also been convicted of sexually assaulting a seven-year-old girl. A coldness opened inside me, and I turned to the teacher next to me, who had young children.

"How old is a child when he's in second grade?"

"Seven."

"That's what I was afraid of."

NINE

Jevon's last visit to Mr. Hudson's office was precipitated by an altercation involving his cousin, Oron. Oron was a senior at Greenville High School, seven months away from graduating. Oron dressed well. His shirts and pants were always clean and ironed, his shoes freshly shined, and his fingers and neck were adorned with the gold jewelry that many black teenagers of his generation appreciate. Oron always addressed me as "sir" in the hallway even though he didn't know me. He was immersed in a number of school activities and most faculty members accorded him the trust of a fellow adult. If something important needed to be done, a faculty member could send Oron to do it without ever worrying that he would detour to the gymnasium or poke his head into someone else's classroom. He was also unusual because he showed an old-fashioned respect for female students, never engaging in the flirtatious banter that characterized most of the conversations at Greenville High.

For several weeks he had been harassed by a group of boys who lived down the street from him. He was not tormented in the way that awkward kids are teased in gym class, but harassed the way that civil rights marchers were once molested by angry mobs: an ugliness that flirts dangerously with violence, an anger threatening always to become evil. Twice he had been chased home, once beaten up, and threatened with much worse. The perpetrators were a group of thugs that ran with the Eighth Street Boys, a small makeshift gang of cousins and neighbors who lived, not surprisingly, on Eighth Street. Their dislike for Oron seemed to be that his decency made their own depravity all the more obvious. Oron took French II with one of these boys, a bully the other students called Debo, and despite continual harassment before, during, and after class, Oron maintained a principled aloofness, and excelled in the class.

Oron's life changed course forever on a Friday night at a Greenville High football game. I was also at the game, but along with most of the other two thousand people, I was oblivious to what happened to Oron that night.

Behind the Greenville High School football stadium one can see all the tenuous steel girders that hold the bleachers up, and everyone must pass underneath those bleachers to get to the seats. The area is dank and dimly lit and is a kids' domain. A teacher passing through is greeted by a legion of uncomfortable smiles concealing some offense. The offenses can be as innocent as an accidental swear word or as sordid as alcohol, drugs, and fighting. As in any town, many kids who come to the game never even see the field, but come to scurry back and forth under the bleachers.

On that night, Oron was cornered in that shadowy underground while hundreds of adults sat only a few feet above him, eating popcorn and trying to figure out which of the five offensive linemen was actually their son. Oron was carrying popcorn and a Coke back from the concession stand when Debo and two of his henchmen came up behind him. They were upon him before he had time to act, hitting and kicking him with furious blows. He was hurt seriously enough that he could not muster the strength to resist while his attackers ripped the rings off his fingers, snatched his watch, and tore the necklaces from around his neck.

The story that pulsed through the school on Monday was about a fellow teacher who had found two students smoking behind the gym and asked them to put out their cigarettes. As he pressed his case, one of the students cold-cocked him in the back of the head, knocking him to the ground. Without his glasses, the teacher was left defenseless and the boys ran off. All the perpetrators escaped. By Monday, everyone—including myself—seemed to know who had done it, but nothing ever came of it.

This gruesome story monopolized the hallways Monday morning, so we were deep into second block before reports began circulating about what had happened to Oron. Third block had just begun when Jevon, from my second-block class, knocked on my door. I opened the door quizzically, knowing that he was supposed to be in French II. In a deadpan voice, he asked if he could borrow some paper towels. I walked over to my desk and ripped him off two paper towels. Before I made it back to the doorway he stopped me.

"No," he said, "I need the whole roll."

"What do you need the whole roll for?" I asked skeptically.

"Kid's head's busted open all over the floor, blood's everywhere down there. We need some paper towels."

I handed him the paper towels without comment. Had I not been preoccupied with the shock waves that erupted in my own room I would have gone with him.

By lunch I had heard the whole story. When Oron arrived to French class, Debo was already in the room, seated at Oron's desk prominently displaying the jewelry he had stolen from Oron three days before. The necklace and the rings were obvious, the bracelet only slightly concealed beneath a shirtsleeve. Oron remained silent, but walked quietly over to where Jevon was sitting. They conversed for a moment until the bell rang, and the last students arrived to take their seats. Ms. Coris closed the door and proceeded to write the morning's first assignment on the board.

Without warning, Oron picked up a wooden stool encased in metal. His face lit with rage and he clubbed the back of Debo's head with the stool. The first blow knocked Debo out of his chair, cracking his head and spraying blood all over the three desks in front of him. Once the boy was on the ground Oron stood over him and swung again, and still again, this time striking Debo's head with such force that the stool shattered into pieces. By now Ms. Coris was shrieking for security. The students stared in horror, all except for Jevon, who stood in front of the two boys to make sure no one interfered.

As the blood streamed out of Debo's head, Oron snatched the pieces of the stool, the broken legs and top, and alternately smashed them across the defenseless body on the floor. Oron broke the scraps of chair into smaller and smaller pieces across his victim's face, and once they disintegrated into splinters, he pummeled Debo—now unconscious—with his bare hands. In the midst of his tirade Oron caught sight of the security guards appearing at the door.

"Come on!" he screamed. "Who's next? Fuck all of you. Bring the fuckin' security! Come on, I'll give you more than you want."

The guards backed away. They radioed for Mr. Hudson, who appeared in an instant, then called for the police.

"Bring it on, Mr. Hudson!" Oron shouted once he appeared. "Come on, Mr. Hudson, I'll fuckin' kill all of you."

Mr. Hudson remained calm and—as was his gift—eventually lured Oron out of the room and into custody.

When the ambulance arrived to carry Debo out the back door, Oron was being ushered out the front door, handcuffed and in police custody. His shoes were shined, his designer shirt well-ironed and still tucked in, though now drenched heavily with blood. Debo was hospitalized in intensive care for over a week with a fractured skull. He returned to school a couple of weeks later, still wearing Oron's jewelry. Oron never returned to Greenville High School.

Sometime later I ran into Corelle Wright at a local catfish stand, where he was picking up some food for his infant son. He made no pretense about returning to school or planning to get his GED. We visited for a moment as he waited for his food, his feet shifting rapidly and his eyes tracing the cracks in the linoleum floor. When they handed him his food he smiled meekly, then brushed by me, and slid out the door.

Corelle's favorite part of English II had been a play we read by August Wilson, *The Piano Lesson.* Every time I have taught *The Piano Lesson* since, visions of Corelle have come rushing back through the character of the wayward but lovable Boy Willie. In one long monologue, Boy Willie talks about the turning point in his life, the terrifying moment when he confronted the world's opinion of his own uselessness:

> Many is the time I looked at my daddy and seen him staring off at his hands. I got a little older and I knew what he was thinking. He sitting there saying, "I got these big ol' hands but what I'm gonna do with 'em? Best I can do is make a fifty-acre crop for Mr. Stovall. All I got is these hands. Unless I go out here and kill somebody and take what he got . . . it's a mighty long row to hoe for me to get something of my own. So what I'm gonna do with these big ol' hands?"

It is the growing perception of their own uselessness—together with the apparent lawlessness of the world around them—that hurtles boys like Corelle, Larry, Jevon, and Oron toward extinction. Corelle is only twenty-two years old now, and twice that number of years remains for him to sit in his house and gaze at his powerful hands the way Boy Willie's father did, wondering why they have become so useless. Right now America's hope is that Corelle will fill those hands with something other than a gun. But if Corelle is denied his place for too long, he, like Boy Willie, may one day come to believe that the only way to make the world look you in the eye is by pointing a gun at it.

Part Three

LIFE, DEATH, AND IMMORTALITY

AT GREENVILLE HIGH

TEN

It was just a regular Monday until I arrived at the office to sign in at 7:30. I had been in Lula, Mississippi, visiting friends on Saturday, and had been barricaded in my house all day Sunday to grade papers. I was writing an announcement to place next to the microphone when I overheard the secretary's conversation with two female students leaning over the counter.

"When's the funeral gonna be?" one asked.

"The family hasn't decided yet," the other said. "And she was just starting to get everything together. . . ."

As I stopped what I was doing and looked at the two girls and the secretary, the gravity of the morning suddenly became apparent. The office was moving as if underwater, the regular hustle and bustle had slowed to a stillness of protest, a refusal to go back to the little things. Nervous for the answer, I asked the girls what had happened.

"A student got killed Saturday night on Nelson Street."

Home to most of Greenville's after-hours clubs, curbside gambling, and drive-by shootings, Nelson Street was unequivocally the most dangerous spot in Greenville. There is no phrase in the Greenville lexicon that connotes trouble as much as Nelson Street. It is a phrase every parent knows and fears; most times it is the last instruction given to any child as he or she leaves the house: "Now stay off Nelson, you hear me?" Nonetheless, its promise of sin attracts youngsters en masse.

"Who was it?" I asked anxiously.

"Egina Dickens," she responded.

I leaned heavily on top of the copier machine. Gina? I thought. Gina, what the hell were you doing on Nelson Street?

The girl responded as if she heard my silent question.

"She had just got off work at Garfield's, and was just heading over there to Floree's to get some food. You know they got food in there too, next to the club part. She was just walking in the door to the club when some crazy dude started shooting. They was throwing dice out there, and I guess he lost a whole lot of dough, and the boy that walked away with it was going into the club too, so he just started shooting towards the doorway, two guns at once. Didn't hit that boy he was shooting for, but hit Gina right in the back of the head."

Gina was always at Garfield's on weekend nights; she was the hostess. That was where I had first met her. She must not have left there until after one, because the restaurant serves until midnight. I watched through the glass as students gathered outside the door. I looked down at the Chess Club announcement I was halfway through, and dropped it in the trash.

The morning announcements came on minutes later when I was walking down the hall. Because the reception was so bad in many parts of the hallway, I stepped into the counselor's office so I could hear them. One of my students was sitting right inside the door but I did not say hello. Two students sitting across from me were crying; we exchanged glances but did not speak. Instead, I sat down on the floor, put my head in my hands, leaned quietly against the wall, and waited for Mr. Hudson's voice.

"We would like to, as a school, share a moment of silence for Egina Dickens, who we lost this weekend." Around the school, conversations stopped, feet ceased to shuffle, coats and backpacks remained steadfastly silent. The students next to me sobbed with a tender patience—their slow, pendulous tears proving that this was neither the first nor the last time.

Because she was a senior and I taught mostly sophomores and juniors, I hadn't taught Egina. Nonetheless, she was one of the handful of students who had sought me out as a friend despite the absence of a formal teacher-student relationship. Short and petite, Gina was graceful, with a quick and contagious smile, a dark-skinned girl who was one of the school's most attractive young women. The first time I met her at Garfield's she immediately struck me as confident, gracious, and charismatic—I was sure she was older than I was. She was beautiful in the grandest sense, possessing a kind of beauty that filled a room and made it easier to live in. Her presence seemed too powerful to disappear.

I wondered about the rest of the day. Certainly it could not continue as a regular school day—this was a distraction too significant to be ignored, and almost too difficult to be taken on directly. Then I remembered that Egina's only sibling, Melinda, was in my second-block class. Had she come to school today? What would I tell her? Should I go ahead with the lesson on commas if she was there?

I looked at the clock; seventy minutes remained until the start of second block. Sometime later I heard the bell ring and the distant thundering of eleven hundred students rustling books and pencils, and pairs of feet shuffling, stopping, searching. The first student to enter my room was Timothy. For the first time all year, I said nothing to him. Students trickled in, a couple at a time, none of us looking each other in the eye, as if each one of us had been there, had pulled the trigger. Finally the halls cleared and I closed the door: no Melinda. Instead of the raucous interchange of laughs and gossip that usually accompanied this group's entrance, there was an expectant silence. Pairs of eyes watched me, elbows leaning over the front of desks, waiting, perhaps for the first time, for me to tell them what to do. There was a very small number of correct answers that I could give, and commas certainly wouldn't be one of them. "Let's circle up the desks," I said. "I want to talk about Gina."

There was at first a good deal of head shaking, general grief and uncertainty, but the fifteen accounts and interpretations of the weekend that filled the room eventually gave way to one voice. It was the voice I would have chosen to speak. Perhaps the most insightful student in the class, Julian Wyatt was originally from Chicago, and his brother was serving fifteen years for cocaine trafficking. He was a student who, in a different school, might have been the homecoming king and every mother's dream—a gifted athlete, good-looking, and smart. But at Greenville Julian ran with the Vicelords gang and revealed his intelligence only in sporadic installments to avoid anyone tagging him as "smart." Only three days after I taught Julian how to play chess he had fought me to a stalemate.

Julian told us that he was on Nelson Street Saturday night when Egina was killed; he was perhaps the last person to speak to her. He was also a part of the dice game that caused the argument that ignited the shooting.

It was after 1:30 in the morning when Egina got off work and her boyfriend Junebug had come to pick her up. They were headed home but Gina was hungry, and the only place to get food after Garfield's closed was Floree's Lounge. Floree's was primarily a nightclub and juke joint, but consistently attracted a rowdy group of patrons who liked to gamble, use drugs, and tended to carry weapons. To buttress the various activities of the club's patrons, there were some tables in the back where people could get food at all hours of the night. Nelson Street, as Julian put it, "is where

Greenville is bought and sold. People think there's money down on those gambling boats, but they can't touch Nelson." Five of the fifteen tenth graders in my class had been in or by Floree's Lounge the night of Gina's death.

After she got out of her car, Gina stopped to talk with Julian and some of the other boys who were throwing dice on the street corner. Julian said that he was not actually playing, but watching— Gina and Julian visited for only a moment and then she walked toward the entrance. On the other side of the car, a local thug named Toothpick was trying desperately to recoup the money he had lost. The seven that landed against the curb as Gina approached the entrance meant the loss of another several thousand dollars. As the winner picked up the cash and began to move swiftly away, Toothpick mumbled angry expletives and then pulled two handguns from his belt. The man with the money heard his threats and darted past Egina toward the doorway. As he was clearing the doorway, Toothpick began screaming and firing both weapons toward the lounge entrance. The dice game split and people scattered for cover; Julian dove over the car and took off running down the street. In the entryway to Floree's, the bouncer and the doorman dove to the ground; the intended target slid through the doorway and tumbled safely into a corner. A stray bullet struck the back of Egina's head and she collapsed onto the sidewalk, killing her almost instantly. Junebug, a high school dropout and one-time gangbanger, ran to Gina's body, weeping and screaming inconsolably as the life bled steadily out of her.

By the time the ambulance arrived, some fifteen minutes later, Gina's blood had filled the sidewalk outside Floree's and was dribbling over the curb and into the gutter. She was pronounced dead at the hospital, while Melinda and her mom were still in bed. Julian said he didn't know where he was when he stopped running. I imagined him in a furious sprint, not caring that he didn't look tough, but running with the conviction of a fifteen-year-old who knows he wants to drive a car and graduate from high school and even fall in love before a bullet catches him.

Everybody knew who killed Gina. Toothpick was a regular on Nelson, usually riding an old bicycle, asking for money or scamming drugs. His dual commitments to drugs and gambling kept an erratic stream of money hemorrhaging in and out of his possession. He had been in jail twice already, and the black community in Greenville screamed for his arrest. His sister appeared on the evening news and agreed to help hunt for him. Although Gina did not run with a gang, her friends did, and Toothpick's sister probably knew that it was better for the police to find her brother before the Vicelords did.

There was an atmosphere in the high school that day that I had never seen before or since. No one jumped and hollered in the hallways, no one banged on lockers or slapped playfully at friends passing in the halls. Girls walked hand in hand, and many stopped and hugged for long periods of time without speaking or moving. Boys walked somberly. Instead of greetings of, "Yo, what up, dog?" and intricately choreographed handshake-dance routines, they offered a listless nod of the head and an apathetic wave.

Around 10 A.M. Mr. Hudson announced over the loudspeaker that a number of local preachers had been invited to the auditorium, and any students who wished to speak to them could report there. For the first time there were no criteria that followed for who would be allowed to go, or what series of hall passes and formal clearance slips a student would need, or any discussion of what the punishment would be for those attempting to take advantage of the opportunity to walk the halls. For the first time, GHS faculty and staff extended to students the trust of a family. When the announcement ended my students looked at me, stupefied.

"What good's listening to some ol' preacher talk about heaven and hell and all that mess who don't even know Gina?" one said. "I ain't fixing to go down there."

Not surprisingly, it was not those closest to Gina who went to the auditorium, but the peripheral students who wanted to play some active part in a drama that was not explicitly theirs.

By Tuesday Gina's loss had begun to evaporate. The mayhem was back in the hallways and the bustle of Greenville High School seemed to indicate that although she had not yet been laid to rest, Egina Dickens had already gone.

As much out of my own need for grieving as out of my indignation at the absence of any recognition, I went about organizing a memorial for Egina. I found a one-by-two-inch photograph of her in the yearbook archives and drove it to a nearby copy shop to have it blown up to poster size. I gathered some students to create a banner while I bought two hundred grievance cards from Wal-Mart and distributed them to all the seniors Wednesday morning during homeroom. I picked flowers from my neighbor's yard, pulled the mattress pad off my bed and laid it down in the front hallway, covered it with the flowers, hung the photograph and the banner overhead, and waited for students to bring the cards. When the bell rang for second block that day, I was still standing at the makeshift memorial and the crowd was so large that no one could pass through the entryway.

By the time I made it to my room, my second-block class had already arrived. Sitting behind the door, already at the computer, was Melinda, Egina's sister. I could see in her classmates' faces the same rush of anxiety that I felt at the sight of her. Melinda and Egina had different fathers, and this was evident in her body type and facial structure—Melinda was short and thick-boned with a round face. Melinda, nicknamed "Pooh," was obstinate, quick-witted, vociferous and often vulgar, but still charming.

She had one close friend in the class, Latreesha. If they sat together, they talked incessantly. If I separated them, they harassed each other from opposite sides of the room, calling out playful insults about the three topics most likely to be the source of ridicule among many teenage black girls: their mothers, their men, and their hair. Latreesha, Melinda's friend, was every bit as outspoken as Melinda but less tactful. I worried that she lacked the subtlety this situation might require, but it was she who carried Melinda—and the rest of us—through that first day together. Treesha gave me a look as if to say, "Don't worry, I'll take care of it," and latched on to Melinda as if she were the new girl at preschool.

But before class began, I took Melinda into the hall to speak privately with her. The first thing I did, which went against all the professional advice I had received, was to give her a hug. Often adulthood is the hardest lesson of adolescence, and in order for it to seem a lesson worth learning, a child must occasionally see the humanity in it. She must be convinced that it is not entirely devoid of the simple pleasantries and profound affections that mark the childhood she is asked to leave behind.

My neighbor's flowers held their form for the remainder of the week and the cards and photographs overflowed the mattress pad. In each of my classes we wrote letters to Gina and her family and for a few days I let Melinda play solitaire on the computer instead of reading.

Gina was buried on Saturday. I missed the funeral because I had to take my track team to the North State track meet, an inconvenience that was perhaps harder on them than on me. One of the boys on the track team had dated Egina for nearly a year and another had grown up with her as a neighbor.

It was late afternoon that day when I met with our runners for the 4 × 400-relay. I noticed Reginald—whom we called "Hawk"— looking pensively into the distance as I spoke. I paused to get his attention, or to see if he had something to say.

Without moving he muttered, "I bet they're burying Gina right now."

The other boys turned to him for a moment and then bowed their heads. For a moment I wondered if we should have skipped the meet and attended her funeral, but most of our boys were seniors and they had a chance to do something special. I remained silent and waited for one of them to take the lead. It was Hawk again: "We missed the funeral," Hawk said. "All we can do is run for her."

By graduation it seemed like it all had been a ghastly dream. Gina was scarcely mentioned at the ceremony. I remember because I stood with her mother and Melinda through the whole event. Gina's mother was impeccably dressed, although distracted, standing on tiptoe and craning her neck as if a better view might reveal her daughter seated somewhere among the long rows of black gowns. The only reference to Gina came during a brief moment before the diplomas were passed out. The salutatorian asked the crowd to join her in a moment of silence for those seniors who could not be with us. I braced myself for the memories of Egina that I expected to hear from the speaker, and I watched Gina's mother shift her feet while Melinda stared off toward the bleachers. What followed instead was a list of seven students from the class of 1998 who had died over the years. I had to focus hard just to pick out Gina's name.

The staggering tragedy that the school had endured after Gina's death was in fact nothing more than the next installment in a series. These students had been through more memorials than grade promotions, more funerals than honor roll assemblies. Who were the other six? How quickly would Gina's memory descend behind them, like yesterday's sunset, beautiful but gone? Gina's mother fiddled with her purse and walked past me to the door.

Two months later, in two subsequent nights in July, two more Greenville High School students were killed: Anthony Giles and Clifton Anthony. Both deaths were gang-related. Anthony was killed just off Nelson Street in a shoot-out that ensued after a minor scuffle between his boys from the Eighth Street gang and a few members of the Ohio-Mulberry Posse. Some students of mine who knew Anthony well, and one who was with him that night, swore that one of Anthony's own boys shot him in the back by accident. Nonetheless, his death merited revenge, so his friends from Eighth Street organized a drive-by through OMP territory the following night. Clifton was killed because he was standing on the porch when the drive-by skidded through the neighborhood seeking retribution. He was a student in my Greek mythology class and a member of my chess club.

Not surprisingly, no arrest was made for Anthony's murder. Tavius, the boy arrested for Clifton's murder, was also a student at Greenville High, and after testifying against some of the police's more notorious targets, he was released and reenrolled at Greenville High just three weeks after school started. Tavius spent that semester as a student in my Greek mythology class and also in the second-block algebra II class next door to me. Also in that class was Pierre Anthony, Clifton's only brother.

Because Clifton's and Anthony's deaths occurred in the summer, Greenville High held no memorial for them. Whenever I mentioned Clifton or Anthony, students' faces darkened with the memory of unhealed wounds. From Clifton and Gina and countless others before them, students had absorbed the lesson of their own expendability, sensing that their lives might amount to little more than an ephemeral whisper lodged somewhere between the "color guard" and the "diplomas" at graduation.

Except for a classmate at Yale who had been killed by a drunk driver, Gina was the first young person I had known who died. In its own numbing way it prepared me for the deaths of Anthony and Clifton, and their deaths inoculated me against anything else the Delta could offer. Once enough days of normalcy had passed over the graves of Egina and Clifton and Anthony, and the loss began to wear off, the Delta I lived in began to take a different shape. Their deaths had raised the stakes of despair. Once you've seen the obliteration of a young life, the neglect and deprivation of it—although terrible—no longer stirs your soul the way it once did. I no longer wince at the sight of 120 kids sitting in the gym for two hours with nothing to do; I am no longer heartbroken at the news of another pregnant student or a new familiar name on the drop-out list. In Greenville's black community, like all troubled, impoverished communities with high death rates, there is an accepted lower standard for the quality of life. Those who live, regardless of how they live, already possess one invaluable gift. Anything more is good fortune.

After my first year I saw Pierre and Melinda infrequently; Melinda would stop by to visit or talk to other students; Pierre would stop by to play chess. But each visit's poignant reminder of loss was only that, a memo to the heart. I wondered how many of those memos I could collect before I started to lose track of them, before their urgency slipped quietly away. Growing up in a world where death came seldom, love came easily. In this new place where death came easily, love was a carefully calculated risk.

In some odd way, this understanding brought me closer to the world my students inhabited, and with this new intimacy came new information. Soon, rarely a week passed that I did not sit with a child to discuss the death of a father or an uncle or a cousin or a close friend. When a fellow teacher stopped me at my mailbox to tell me to keep an eye on Reggie, because his father had been murdered over the weekend, I stopped to say I was sorry, picked up my mail, and hurried to class as the bell was ringing. I would keep an eye on Reggie, but he was not alone.

ELEVEN

Somewhere in the mayhem of the first two weeks I taught at Greenville High School, I had volunteered to host English tutoring. The tutoring was primarily intended for students who had missed class due to absence and needed to make up work. However, most of the students who had missed school either didn't care, or didn't care until the last week of the semester when they finally realized they would fail the course if they did not make up their work. As a result I spent most of these "tutoring" sessions grading papers by myself, except for the days that Dianca came.

I knew it was going to be another day of empty tutoring when the voices in the hallways had slowed to the sporadic hollering of a few cheerleaders practicing their routines, and still no one had arrived in my room. So I sat down at my desk for the first time all day and began sifting through a stack of essays. I do not know how long Dianca was peeking in my door before I noticed her. When I looked up, her face erupted into a joyous smile and she began to laugh the way a toddler laughs at a parent's tickling.

"You didn't even know I was there, didya?" she asked.

"No," I responded. "How long have you been standing there?"

"Fuh the longest, a few minutes, I just be fooling with ya."

"Are you here for English tutoring?" I asked.

"Sho' am, I was getting me some assignments from Ms. Jones."

"I'm Mr. Johnston."

"I know. I'm Dianca Green."

"Pleasure to meet you, Dianca."

She crossed over and deposited a prodigious stack of papers and books on top of my desk.

"Wow! Is that all your makeup work?" I asked.

"Sho' is. I got two weeks I got to make up," she sighed.

"Two weeks? We've only been in school four weeks. You only come to school every other day?"

"I wish," Dianca laughed. "I was fixing to have my baby the day before school started so I stayed right at home. I didn't end up having him 'til the twelfth of August, but I sho' thought he was fixing to come every one of them days. I just got back a week and a half ago."

Dianca was the first Greenville High student I met who had a child. Her tone was surprisingly unapologetic—in fact, proud—as if we were both thirty years old and sitting in an office discussing the families we were raising.

"Is it a boy or a girl?" I asked.

"A boy, his name's DJ. Ooh, and he be bad already. He don't sleep fuh nothing, waking me up all the time. Most of the time he don't even want nothing, he just want to wake me up so I got to be woke too."

"Who takes care of him while you're at school? He's too young to go to some sort of day care, right?"

"Yeah, my mom stay with him on days she ain't working. When she be working my auntie take him."

"Well," I said. "Let's take a look at some of this work you got."

Dianca had massive piles of work in history and math, but I helped her mostly with her English I class. Although she was a sophomore, she had failed English I in her freshman year and had to make it up this fall. She came every Monday, Tuesday, and Thursday to tutoring—and was usually the only student there.

Over the course of those afternoons Dianca and I came to be good friends. Eventually I was quite comfortable talking with her about DJ and the world of motherhood. Most of our sessions were occupied equally by my questions about being a parent and her questions about English. From Dianca I learned to recognize the scores of girls in Greenville High who were in various stages of childbearing and child rearing. I knew to look for shirts that weren't tucked in, baggy clothing, a shape of plumpness that was just mildly out of proportion with a sixteen-year-old body, keychains with baby photographs.

The more keen my eye became, the more I learned about the lives of female students with children. The lives differed with the personalities: on a Tuesday Annette went directly from her second-block class to the hospital and gave birth. She was back in school by Friday and in four years never missed a quarter on the honor roll. Takeisha was pregnant with her second child in the middle of her sophomore year; in the months before the birth she did nothing in any of her classes, including mine. When she left school for the birth, she never returned. The most interesting compromise perhaps was Sonya's, who was plagued by morning sickness throughout the early months of her pregnancy. She was so reluctant to miss school that her teacher and classmates agreed to let her bring her own trash can into first block. If she got sick, she got sick, but in her words, she "never missed that lesson."

The more of these students I observed, the more curious I grew about Dianca's story, since she was the mother I knew best. Dianca possessed a maturity that made our conversations comfortable even when they trod on very personal ground. It was the end of a long working afternoon when she began, unsolicited, to talk about DJ's father.

"DJ daddy be calling me all the time wanting to see DJ, he's good like that, I give him that. We quit talking not too long after DJ was born. It wasn't because DJ was born, but we just wasn't getting along so good. He wanted to start having sex again right after DJ born. I told that boy he must be crazy. He just don't know what a woman body got to go through, I just wasn't ready for all that."

"What did he say when you first told him you were pregnant?"

"He was all right, he say he love to have a little DJ running around. His name's DJ too."

"What about you, what was your reaction when you first knew?"

"Well, when I knew for real? I been wondering for a while, thinking I might be, so I be thinking about it a lot. I don't too much know what I thought, I wasn't too much happy or sad, it just be the way it is. I s'pose I knew it might happen when we started having sex, but I just sorta hoped it wouldn't."

"Were you using some sort of protection?"

"Nah, I thought about it, but we never really did too much use nothing."

"What about your parents? What'd they say."

"My dad be furious, he went to clowning for real! But he don't stay with us, so that don't too much matter. My mom just shook her head then said, 'Well, D, what we gonna do?' She ask me if I thought about abortion at all. I said I didn't see no reason for to kill my baby 'cause a what I did. You grown enough to lay down you grown enough to deal with the consequences. There sho' was times when I wisht I hadn't had him. When he was first born I couldn't do nothing but sit right there with him all da time, fixing him and feeding him and cleaning him up and listening to him holler and trying to make him shut up even when he ain't hollering for no good reason. Can't go out with friends, can't even much talk on the phone with nobody 'cause you know he gonna start hollering about something and I got to go fuss with him. I s'pose that's probably why his daddy and I quit talking. I didn't have no time."

"How could you manage schoolwork and everything else?"

"Now it be different, we get along a little better. He know some of my friends so if I want to go to somebody house or go kick it with some friends he be straight with that, I can take him with me. Then if he start acting crazy I can give him to one of my friends or sumt'n, see if he calm down. We straight now. All these boys say they don't want to talk to no girls that got kids but that ain't really true neither. A lot of 'em want to talk to you just *because* you got a kid, they figure if you got a kid then you gave it up before, they's a pretty good chance you gonna give it up again. Plus all these girls round here got kids now, can't hardly talk to somebody without them having a kid. That go for boys too, most of these boys round here somebody's daddy, now they gonna say, 'It ain't mine,' as soon as somebody tell 'em they pregnant, but it be theirs. The girl, she know.

"Some of these girls have a kid, boys know she got a kid, so ol' girl will just go on and start sleeping with anybody that stop long enough to take her clothes off. I guess she figured she done messed up already, ain't no sense in trying to be a churchgoer, everybody know. Next thing you know they got three, four kids and flunked out of high school. Other girls, they get one kid and they lock themselves in the house, don't never go near no boys no more, act just like they grown. Don't go to church for those months they pregnant, then after that child born, they show up again try and pretend nothing happened.

"Other than that ain't much you can do. Everybody know you got that kid, dem good boys think you a rat, and the nasty boys wanna make sho' you is a rat so they can get themselves some. First time you talk to a boy he wanna throw you in the bed. If you say no, he gonna say, 'What up? You gonna lay down for somebody else but you ain't gonna lay down fuh me?' Less you want to go along wit dat, you stay at home with yo' mama and auntie watching Jerry Springer."

"So which one are you, the one staying home and watching Jerry Springer?"

Dianca laughed her riotous laugh, throwing her head back and cackling, "I don't know Mr. J., but I can tell you I sho' ain't gonna be the one with three or four kids dropped out of high school. I know I ain't gonna be that one, you and I gonna make sure I ain't that one."

"That's a deal."

Dianca made up all her assignments and passed all her classes that fall. After Christmas I was pleased to discover that she would be in my second-block English II class. Although she was often the source of disruptive laughter or a side conversation, her exuberance extended into the work she did in class. She worked hard, and although some things did not come easily, she persevered with great discipline. On occasion Dianca would bring up DJ or some aspect of motherhood in relation to a class discussion, often edifying and entertaining the rest of the room, including myself.

One morning we were discussing an African folk tale in which a woman gives birth to six children, all of whom are stillborn. The witch doctor convinces the mother that each stillborn child is actually the same original child who has come back to haunt her. The doctor encourages her to smash the sixth dead child's bones; instead the mother simply marks the behind of the corpse with an X and buries him. When the seventh child is born, she turns him over and sees the same X on his behind. One of the midwives tries to justify this impossible occurrence by arguing that it might be a scratch caused by the placenta.

As the students were engrossed in the rich mystery of this story, a series of hands shot up in the air to ask if a placenta was some sort of dark witchcraft. I began to stumble through an explanation, exposing my relative ignorance about the topic.

Before I continued much further, Dianca blurted out: "I tell you what it is!" She proceeded to explain in great detail what exactly a placenta was and what role it played in the birthing process. The students were fascinated by Dianca's story, and for several minutes I stood back as they directed questions at her.

Dianca's leadership in that early instance proved useful not only in explaining to the class—and to me—the role of the placenta, but also in communicating to the other students the sense that their stories mattered too. We listened to Julian's story about playing Russian roulette at age ten, how he watched curiously the boy who hesitated to pull the trigger when he knew the bullet was in the chamber, and winced at the bang and the sight of that young boy's head emptying onto the pavement, as Julian sat, too afraid to move, and waited for the police to come. Another time Julian shared a story about the day the police came to arrest his brother for a cocaine charge, and we listened as he tried to describe the feeling of giving your brother away to a "great steel monster" that will not return him for fifteen years. We listened to Trevor tell us the story about his cousin, Bobby, who had slept in a bed with him for more than ten years. We waited as Trevor swallowed hard to tell us about the moment he rounded the corner from a trip to the store and watched as Bobby burned to death inside the house they had shared. We heard him promise that if his mother would only have let him, he would have sprinted into that crackling inferno to bring his cousin out. We heard the story of the birth of Dianca's son, the burial of Melinda's sister, the murder of Timothy's uncle as Tim sat nestled in the backseat of a car watching a strange man pump his uncle full of shotgun shells.

When the stories grew too heavy, Dianca would chime in with some levity about DJ's antics to ease the strain in the room.

Dianca's goodness and her sensitivity led her to be a leader among that class even as she struggled with the classwork. But Dianca had common sense and she worked hard. She enjoyed success in a way that makes teachers feel validated, if only for a moment. Whenever she would grasp a concept that had proved difficult, a smile would spread so wide across her face that her eyes would nearly close, and she would laugh.

There was something deeply triumphant about her laugh, and yet it was laced with a distant note of despair. Her laugh proclaimed: "Who would have thought Dianca Green would ever know the difference between an independent and a subordinate clause?" It was a momentary triumph over the incessant expectation of defeat.

There were only eighteen students in Dianca's class. In addition to Dianca, by February the other parents included Trevor, who was the father of twin sons; Demetria, who was six months pregnant; Latonya, who was three months pregnant; and Jamie, who had a one-year-old. Tanya became both the most surprising and the most disappointing student in that class. She was one of Greenville High's model students. Each class has a handful of leaders, male and female, who distinguish themselves among their peers. Often for boys this distinction requires a certain dose of athleticism, intelligence, popularity, and good looks, or some combination of the four. For girls this distinction seems to demand attractiveness, popularity, manners, and intelligence, often in that order of importance. Pretty and popular, Tanya was kind and always well behaved. She sat in the front row, and although work was not easy for her, she was always on task. Tanya's mother was a principal in a school in Hollandale, which in itself did much to ensure her good behavior.

On the first day of class Tanya told me that she wanted to go to Howard University. It was the first time that I had ever heard a

Greenville High student openly express an ambition to attend a competitive national university. I assumed that she would exhibit a work ethic and a curiosity to match her ambition, but she did not. She regularly scored middle to low Bs, and even these were on essays and tests that showed no striking signs of creativity or independent thinking. Nonetheless, she always did her best to keep up with her work and always seemed a decent and composed young woman.

Tanya sat next to Dianca and over the course of the semester they became good friends. In every free moment their heads leaned together for furtive conferences, whispers occasionally interjected by a boisterous laugh or a muffled snicker. Several times I had to break up the conversations when I passed by and realized they were inappropriate. The inappropriate subjects were always the same: boys and sex.

The first time I noticed that Tanya was in the midst of a real adolescent struggle came in an essay she wrote about the difficulties facing teenagers. Tanya wrote about girls getting involved with boys for the wrong reasons. She discussed how tragic it was that these girls did things they knew were wrong but continued to do them anyway and, worst of all, lied to their parents about them.

Once a semester I would meet with each student for an individual writing conference out in the hall. The students' most recent essay was the one about which I had chosen to hold a conference. Each conference was meant to last about five minutes. Tanya was the second student to come out for her conference, but forty-five minutes later, when the bell rang, we were still talking.

We had been discussing the grammatical points of her essay for a couple of minutes when we stumbled on a sentence about kids having to lie to their parents. Before I finished reading the sentence, Tanya jumped in.

"You know, Mr. Johnston, sometimes there's just no way around lying to your parents. They make you do it."

"Why do you say that, Tanya?" I asked.

Tanya told me she had been dating a boy named Michael who did not go to Greenville High, although he was black. He went to St. Joe's, the Catholic school nestled in Greenville High School's backyard. St. Joe's was the only private or parochial school in Greenville with enough blacks to constitute a significant percentage. The few well-off black families who wanted a better education for their children and were not afraid of censure from the black community sent their children to St. Joe's. Tanya was the first student I had met at Greenville High who had ever mentioned having acquaintances at St. Joe's, let alone close friends or a boyfriend.

"Well, Mr. J., we've been talking for a long time, and he's always just so sweet to me," she continued. "He would buy me nice stuff, or take me to the movies and out for dinner afterwards. Sometimes he would just stop by and give me flowers or a little ring or just anything. He never pushed anything, I mean we were doing stuff a little but we weren't having sex or anything. And then we talked about it a few times and I said I didn't think I was ready, but then he'd bring it up again, always real sweet though. Mr. Johnston, you don't know him. He's cute, he's for-real cute. He could have any girl he wanted, but he wanted me. We had been together for a month or so, it didn't seem like all that much he was asking. He didn't really make me, he just kept asking. There are a hundred girls that would give that to him in a second, and he said that if we didn't sleep together he was going to need to get it from someone else. So I figured if I slept with him he wouldn't leave me. I figured, you know, just once or twice and then it would be okay."

"It didn't turn out like that, though, did it?"

"No. Well, we did it once or twice and I sorta thought that would be it, but he said he wanted us to be as close as we could. 'Cause he could've just left me after I gave it to him. A lot of boys do that, they sleep with you, and then they dump you anyway and talk about you. But he didn't, he stayed with me and he's still interested, and he keeps calling me and taking me out and he hasn't gotten sick of me or anything. Once I had already slept with him, I mean it didn't really seem to matter how many times I did, I knew it was wrong to do but it seemed like it was turning out okay. But I figured that if I suddenly stopped, it would all go bad and he would leave me and tell everybody and then I would feel terrible."

"So what'd you do?"

"Well, I didn't know what to do. So pretty much whenever he calls I'll just go over, or he'll come over if my parents aren't home. But a lot of times I sneak out of the house, and we'll go somewhere. Cause, Mr. Johnston, my parents won't let me do anything, so I have to sneak out the house to go see him. And I end up having to lie to my parents all the time, and that's what I hate. But I have no choice."

"Tanya, it sounds to me like you don't have any interest in being sexually involved with this boy."

"I don't really, I guess I never did. Now it gets to the point where I get nervous every time the phone rings 'cause I know it might be him and he's gonna ask me to meet him someplace. Then I'm gonna have to think up some lie to give to my mom about going over to somebody's house to study, then I'm going to go with Michael and not study. Then if I fail the test the next day, my mom and dad are gonna be disappointed, wondering why I can't pass the test when I spend all this time studying."

"Tanya, if you don't want to be sexually involved with this boy, don't you think that you should tell him that? Isn't that a bigger problem than lying to your parents?"

"But Mr. J., he's better than all the other boys. He's smart and he treats me good, he's got money and he wants to go to college and do something with his life. Those are all things I want from somebody someday."

I could sense that from where Tanya sat, my arguments couldn't touch the real nature of things. When I examined my watch, I noticed that class was nearly over, and I began to feel the urgency of Tanya's dilemma. I feared what might happen if another night passed, and another phone call came, and another compromise was made before Tanya got back to my room.

"First of all, Tanya," I said, "are you using protection?"

"Well, ya . . . well, no. We never do really. We used to sometimes, but we don't really anymore."

"Tanya, you have to do that. You have to do that if you're going to have sex with him again. I don't think you should sleep with him again at all, but if you are, you have to use protection. You want to do so much with your life, but it becomes so much more difficult to do it with a child."

"I know. I know. There's just a lot more to it than that, I can't just up and insist on something like that, it's just not that easy. I mean he has some say in it too, and I know he would never want me to get pregnant or anythin'."

Before I could respond the bell ended our conversation with a harsh clang that called hordes of students into the hallway. As we gathered our things and tried to push our desks back inside the room before chaos overtook us, I managed to tell Tanya that I would like to continue our conversation, perhaps the next day, since we did not get a chance to finish. She avoided my eyes and mumbled quietly, "Yeah, okay."

In the coming weeks I made a number of attempts to reopen the conversation with Tanya, but she was always in a hurry to go somewhere or meet someone and proposed dispassionately that we have the conversation some other time. The way she cast her eyes did more to disappoint me than the absence of our conversation, for it spoke all she had to say: She was doing her best, and at the moment that was all she could do.

In the middle of March, Tanya began to gain some weight. The taut lines that made up the angles of her face rounded and her jagged hips began to fade, growing vague and imprecise. Still, she skirted my invitations to conversation. I watched Tanya carefully, her affect as well as her physique, waiting for them to betray the misfortune that I presumed. Counter to my own expectations, Tanya's size, as well as her anxiety, reached a plateau and then began to diminish. It came and went like a wave that rises, rises, and crashes, leaving remnants of its rise on the beach before it pulls the rest back out to sea.

I gave up the direct pursuit of a conversation, replacing it with tepid inquiries about her family and her happiness, never wanting to strike a wounded area. When I made just such a modest inquiry in April, she seized the opportunity to ask if she could come talk to me after school. I was reading in my empty classroom when she appeared in the doorway. "Mr. Johnston," she said, "I've been wanting to talk to you ever since that conversation we had a few weeks ago, but I've just been so busy."

"Is everything all right?"

"Yes, I guess so. It is now. Michael and I aren't together anymore, we split up a couple of weeks ago." For a moment her countenance passed through mourning, then brightened. "Although I just started talking to an eleventh grader over here at Greenville High. His name's Demarcus."

"I hope that it's a good thing that you and Michael are no longer together."

"Yeah, well it wasn't at the time, but now it is." Her voice strengthened a little as she convinced herself, and then gathered the strength to go on. "Well, the reason I been so weird lately is that, well, I found out about a month ago that I was pregnant. I didn't know what to do or who to tell so I told Michael. He told me that the baby wasn't his, but he's the only boy I ever slept with, I promise, Mr. Johnston."

"Tanya, you don't have to convince me."

"Well I tried to convince him," she continued, "but he say he wasn't gonna stay with a girl who was sleeping around on him. He didn't call for a few weeks and when I called him he was never home, and never called me back. So I had no choice, I had to tell my mom. We both cried and cried; she was furious. She kept talking about college and my wedding, and how was I gonna do it and how she never wanted me to be one of those girls whose own daughter is the flower girl at her wedding."

I nodded, wanting to spare her the ordeal of explaining, but she pressed on.

"I asked her what we were gonna do. She said I should have an abortion. I never wanted to be one of those people that has an abortion but . . . what were my choices? I mean I would have been sixteen with a child, no one to take care of it. I would've had to quit school or my mom woulda had to quit her job. We can't afford that. I can hardly figure out English II, how'm I gonna raise a little child? I don't know anything about kids, except that I'm still a kid myself. When I become a mother someday I want to do it the best that I can, not just do it to get it over with. I don't want to do it like Dianca, I want to do things, have things."

"How about your parents, how are things with them?" I asked.

"Oh, they're good, things are so much better now that this is all over. But I don't think they like my new boyfriend Demarcus too much. I always go over to Dianca's house to call him 'cause he don't like calling my house case my mom or dad answer."

Not knowing what else to say, I nodded my head silently, looking beyond Tanya to the bookshelves and the chalkboard. The notes from the day before were clumsily erased and then written over, shards of their meaning still discernible through these new words, fragments of the past still visible through these new worlds placed over the old.

TWELVE

I turned through the cast-iron gates and guided my truck along the two faint lines of dead grass that bent hard right and circled around to the center of the graveyard. I had come to find the grave of William Alexander Percy.

A local hero to the white community, I knew little of Percy other than his book, *Lanterns on the Levee: Recollections of a Planter's Son.* The book had been recommended to me as a fine introduction to the history and culture of the Delta. Percy's family continues to be a prominent one, and he was Greenville's best tributary to the impressive stream of literature that has emerged from Mississippi in the twentieth century. His grave sat in a family plot guarded by an eight-foot-tall stone soldier regaled with full armor and a sword.

Later, I was fifty yards down the same road when I noticed a wide field scattered with wooden crosses, clumps of stones, and occasional flowers. Because it was devoid of the cast-iron fence and the alabaster and cement headstones, it took me a moment to realize that this was also a cemetery. Mounds of dirt and homemade stones carved with garden tools and old hunting knives marked the graves. This was the black graveyard. I got out of the car and began to examine the markings. The sense of age that touched the white graveyard was present here too, but in a different voice. The black cemetery showed age the way a barn does, a steadfast simplicity weathered by the elements. The white graveyard showed age the way Gothic churches do, through a style made timeless in an effort to connect us to things past, to great ideas and institutions that couldn't be born in the present. My house sat on a narrow strip of space between the two cemeteries: the two worlds of the Delta, bound by the land but divided by the stories that grow upon it, even in death.

The main reasons for the economic disparity of the Delta lie in its history. In the early 1800s, the Delta was largely unsettled wilderness covered by dense forest. Only in subsequent decades, when the unprecedented fertility of its soil was discovered, did the thought arise to clear the land for farming. Those who wished to do so had to be farmers with significant capital and significant strength of labor, because the clearing of each acre required a great deal of work. As a result, the early planters who came to the Delta were extremely wealthy and owned many slaves.

In Washington County, where Greenville is the county seat, the average white family owned eighty-one slaves when the Civil War began.* This meant that after Lee's surrender at the Appomatox Courthouse, the problem of integrating a newly liberated black population in the Delta was especially difficult because the blacks greatly outnumbered the whites. As a result, nervous plantation owners began campaigning for new draconian "Negro laws" to keep the former slaves productive and harmless. Others insisted that the state grant freed blacks some of the liberties that Lincoln had decreed in 1863. As this struggle persisted into the early 1900s, the Ku Klux Klan was making virulent headway in Mississippi,

*James C. Cobb, *The Most Southern Place on Earth: The Mississippi Delta and the Roots of Regional Identity*. Oxford University Press, 1992, p. 8.

and Greenville was on the verge of succumbing to its mob rule. In the midst of this struggle emerged Willam Percy Sr., a well-respected white planter who was also a cautious advocate for blacks and determined to prevent the Klan from ruling the city. His important part in this mediation catapulted him, despite his own recalcitrance, into a vacated United States Senate seat. But despite his accomplishments, it was his son, William Alexander Percy, who would go on to be Greenville's greatest success. William Alexander Percy's grandparents were his most attentive tutors through his early years, steeping him in literature and music, politics and history, flowers and dance. Whether sitting on his front porch listening to his senator father discourse with local celebrities or studying Latin, French, and classic literature with his legion of personal tutors, Percy's childhood was scintillating with academic opportunity.

As he described it, "For eight years—in fact, for twenty-three—a great number of people had been pouring out money, skill, time, devotion, prayers to create something out of me that wouldn't look as if the Lord had slapped it together absentmind-edly. Not Alexander the Great nor Catherine II had been tended by a more noble corps of teachers."

The younger Percy attended Sewanee College in Tennessee, now the University of the South, and later went on to Harvard Law School. He practiced law successfully for a number of years in Greenville, but his legacy would be his writing.

In addition to a legion of poems and short stories, Percy's crowning achievement was *Lanterns on the Levee,* the memoir he wrote late in his life. Percy's memoir was viewed by many as the last great testimony of the Southern aristocrats, whom he described as those whose hearts were set "not on the virtues which make sur-viving possible, but on those which make it worthwhile." For white Greenville, Percy is now something of an icon for the celebrated voice of a maligned era. The local library is named after him, and his photograph hangs reverently above the checkout desk at the Greenville High School library.

It was early in my first year at Greenville High School that I first noticed it. I had returned some books to the school library and was on my way back to my classroom, but two steps out of the library, something caught my eye that I had not seen before. The wall was covered with a series of framed photographic montages of white people. Each frame was about three feet high and two feet wide, and inside the frame were seven or eight photographs of graduating seniors circled around a photograph of one faculty member. Each frame bore the title "Hall of Fame." The Wall of Fame, as I came to call it, consisted of photographs proceeding chronologically from the exit of the library to the edge of the main stairway. Previously I had noticed only the pictures closest to the staircase and had given them little attention. Now I was looking at the same display, but they appeared to be photographs from another school, another era. The year of the frame that caught my eye was 1965. In it were eight neatly cleaned and clothed white students. Their hair and clothing had not yet endured the fashion upheavals of the later sixties and seventies; each head was still conservatively cut and each outfit formal. I walked slowly down the row, keeping an eye on 1965.

There were a number of years missing, but the next one I spotted was 1974. I exhaled a little, comforted by the humanness of this group—one white guy with a prodigious attempt at an Afro, close-fitting and fabulously unflattering clothes, horn-rimmed glasses. At the top right of the frame was a black student with a short Afro. I walked farther down the wall to 1981: four whites, three blacks. The white boys wore the embarrassing mullet haircuts of their day, short in the front and long in the back. One wore a green tuxedo, another a leather jacket covered with zippers. I moved more quickly to 1985, the first official crossover: four blacks, three whites. 1987: five blacks, two whites, one purple tuxedo, one listless cutoff T-shirt. I scanned down to the end of the row and back. 1992, the last white face: smiling, confident, unaware. The last two years, were missing. I went back to 1965 and still earlier to '63 and '62 and a number of the fifties. I walked the entire wall again, then walked it backward. The first black face appeared in 1971, the last white one was in 1992. In Greenville, Mississippi, it had taken nearly twenty years to implement *Brown v. Board of Education* and twenty years to destroy it.

Although the story was written on the wall, I wanted to hear it told, so the first chance I had I went to Virginia Alexander, the school librarian. Ms. Alexander was the most perplexing of all the authority figures at Greenville High School. She was Greenville High School's anachronism, a woman from a lost era. I learned to attribute her enigmatic nature to the gradual extinction of the trait so familiar to Ms. Alexander: grace. At one time she would have been the ideal of the mythic white Mississippi aristocracy: genteel, lovely, intelligent, wealthy. She was the only piece of living history that had seen both Greenville High Schools that appeared on the wall. She arrived in 1967, four years before the school integrated. She was there when the first of the black students arrived in 1971; she witnessed their harassment, neglect, and isolation. Then she saw their numbers grow and their success blossom. She staffed the library in 1975 when Greenville High School earned the second highest score of any high school in the state on a standardized academic assessment. She was present in 1977 when the United States Commission on Civil Rights declared Greenville the model for successful school integration. Then she watched as the first white families moved their kids to private schools or remote white districts, and she watched as several wealthy black families and the rest of the white families gradually followed. She had witnessed the collapse of the literary society and the debate team, the gradual crumbling of the theater company, the foreign language club, and the math club; in their place she saw the first pregnant student, the first on-campus rape, the first round of gunshots.

Soon after Greenville High School announced its integration, a declaration came forth that a new private school would open the following September. Everyone in Greenville knew why it was opening; many whispered, but few protested. Twenty-five years later there are several such schools in Greenville and many of the other Delta towns—here they are known simply as the Delta's "white academies."

Greenville High School was built in the 1950s, when white public schools were objects of community pride. It was placed in the heart of one of Greenville's nicest neighborhoods. Fifty years later, the neighborhood surrounding Greenville High is still quite nice. But black Greenvillians' access to economic resources did not change as rapidly as their access to educational resources, and although working-class black families steadily moved south of the highway and bought houses in neighborhoods not far from the school, they did not purchase the expensive real estate that surrounded the school. Although 99.9 percent of the white families eventually abandoned GHS, many whites who lived in the neighborhood did not choose to move because they had invested in or inherited such expensive property.

What remains is one of Greenville's great ironies: Those white families who still live in the neighborhood have to share it with the eleven hundred students whom they deemed unworthy of sharing a classroom with their own children. What was once an eminently desirable neighborhood, due in part to its accessibility to the high school, was now a neighborhood bound inextricably to the fate of the school that had been abandoned. In the late 1980s, property values surrounding the school began to decline steadily as the school experienced more discipline problems and a higher incidence of crime. More and more white families who had with-drawn from the high school eventually withdrew from the neigh-borhood as well. Gradually, the demographics of the community surrounding the school began to reflect the students within the school. Today a good part of the neighborhood to the north and east of the school is black, although to the west and the south it remains predominantly white.

Once again the whites had retreated and retrenched. Perhaps there were times when they had to wince at the possessions they left behind, mementos too cumbersome to carry in the flight, such as the Greenville High School Hall of Fame from 1965. But here it still hung, ignored more than hated, a remnant of a silent evacuation.

It was during one of our innumerable state testing sessions that I first met Marvin Griffin. In a furor to try to improve test scores, the administration had set aside the first forty-five minutes of the school day for test preparation. Although the ninth grade was the only class to be tested, the entire school was put on hold, sent to homeroom, and forced to wait while math and English teachers scurried from room to room tutoring ninth graders. I was assigned a ninth grade room where I would report each day for forty min-utes. I began the first session with a reading comprehension passage. Reading comprehension tended to be one of the glaring weaknesses of my English II students because they did not read much when they were younger, and the reading they had done in previous schooling had taught them only to search for key words and copy the surrounding phrase. As a result, inference, main idea, and appli-cation questions were very problematic for them. We had forty minutes to work, and I assigned a twenty-five-question reading comprehension section that included four reading passages. By the time I had answered all the students' lingering questions and sat down to look over the section for myself, much of the class was well under way. An answer key had been provided for me, but I wanted to familiarize myself with the passages under discussion, and because they were produced within the district, the answer keys frequently contained errors.

I had just finished the first of the four reading comprehension passages when I noticed that Marvin was looking at me. His pencil was down and his booklet closed; he seemed to be wondering if there was something else he was supposed to be doing. Not sure whether Marvin was one of those quiet boys who did his best and then gave up (he was, after all, sitting in the front row), or one who made Christmas trees out of the computerized answer sheet in defiance, I got up and asked him if he was finished. He nodded his head. I picked up his test booklet and returned to my desk to look it over. I checked his first ten answers with the ones I had completed, and they matched perfectly. I then checked the rest of his answers against the answer key: twenty-five out of twenty-five. For each subsequent test preparation section—without alerting anyone—I used Marvin's paper as the answer sheet, and was never disappointed. He even found the correct answers to questions the district had answered incorrectly.

A month later I was seated at the annual Greenville High School Academic Awards Banquet. A retired professional football player who had graduated from Greenville High School had returned from Jackson to give a short talk, and as I was glancing through the program I saw Marvin's name. He was one of two students in the freshman class who had made the Superintendent's List (an honor recognizing straight As throughout the entire year).

I searched the crowd for Marvin and spotted him easily. He was 6'3" and weighed about 130 pounds. All arms and legs, he was a figure difficult to miss, especially in a room where female award recipients outnumbered male recipients nearly fifteen to one. Marvin was seated with a number of women I had never seen, who appeared to be mother, grandmother, and aunt. I introduced myself and told Marvin's family that I had not taught Marvin formally, but was aware of his intellect and was interested in challenging him to raise his expectations.

A dozen or so students had begun speaking to me about outside reading and many came to visit me on days when I would bring in fresh piles of books from my house. I spent nights clearing my bookshelves of anything that might remotely interest a high school student. I brought in books from my middle school and high school days, and some from my college fiction courses, and by the end of the year I had lent out well over one hundred books, from *Beloved* to *Johnny Tremain*, *King Lear* to *The Pearl*, *Native Son* to *The Hardy Boys*. When Marvin came, he took eight books and proceeded to read most of them in the following weeks.

When Marvin returned the books, he asked me if I would help him prepare for his ACT, the college entrance exam that students in the South often take in place of the SAT. I consented and we set up a schedule for two afternoons a week. Marvin never missed a day, and in the process we became great friends. Marvin was an anomaly at Greenville High School. He used words like "plethora" in conversation, wrote avidly on his own, and would challenge teachers to debates over whether Shakespeare was in fact the greatest writer who ever lived. Marvin also joined the soccer team, and on the way to soccer games he'd challenge me to a grammar quiz on the bus, which he would often win—always remembering, for instance, that one places a comma only after an introductory phrase that is more than four words in length.

Marvin was born in Greenville, in a shotgun trailer on Elizabeth Street. He lived with his mother, his father, and his grandmother. His grandmother could not read, and as such never read to him, but always encouraged him to do well, asking about his grades, congratulating him when he succeeded, comforting him when he did not. At age three Marvin taught himself to read by poring over the handful of utility bills or junk mail or old Dean Koontz books that his mother had lying around the house. Since she was busy working, Marvin's mother had little opportunity to read to him or help him in his academic development. When she arrived home there was only time enough to make dinner and collapse, and perhaps to congratulate Marvin on the new words he had mastered from that day, and fall asleep with her newest novel.

Neither Marvin's mother nor his father had gone to college; in fact, no one in Marvin's family had ever gone to college. It would be safe to say that before Marvin met his teachers at school, he had never interacted with a college graduate. But his mother, father, and grandmother did an outstanding job of raising a gentle, inquisitive, and considerate young man. He always was an extraordinary student. In fact, eighth grade was the first year in which he ever received a B: It was in gym class, because the old gym teacher made it his policy to never give As, although he told Marvin that if he did, Marvin surely would have received one.

In middle school Marvin became interested in science fiction, mostly from cartoons he watched on television and from his mother's old mystery novels, which he had now read in full. Marvin's mother was a ravenous reader, picking up books from friends or the library and devouring them in days. While there was scarcely money for food, let alone for books or trips to museums, Marvin made an early education out of reading whatever his mother was done with. As a result, Marvin started writing. He would sit down on Saturdays and create fantasy stories out of his head. Often he would show them to his mother, after his grandmother passed away when Marvin was in the sixth grade. It was also at this time that Marvin met his best friend Jerry, another student of mine.

Jerry was a much less disciplined student than Marvin but he was equally curious about the world. When they became good friends they adopted a hobby best suited to their own interests and the available resources: walking. Marvin and Jerry would leave the house at nine or ten in the morning on a Saturday or a summer day and start walking, and would not return until dark. With no direction, and no money to spend on anything along the way, the two would walk and talk for hours and hours, sometimes traveling up to twenty miles, often wandering for more than eight hours. While other boys were watching television or playing video games, or hanging out at the mall harassing girls, Marvin and Jerry were walking, inventing fictions, analyzing the world in the pieces that passed between stoplights and corner liquor stores and abandoned industrial parks.

In his ninth-grade year Marvin moved out of his house and began to "stay" with his aunt and uncle. At first I thought it was nothing more than a regional oddity, that all of my students inserted the verb "stay" where I always used the verb "live" ("Mr. Johnston, where do you stay at?" "David stays over on Solomon Street." "Do you stay with your mom or your grandma?"). Later I realized that it was more technically accurate than I had at first assumed. In fact, the connotation of transience was appropriate.

In homes with divorced or unwed parents, the family unit is subject to change much more frequently, regardless of socio-economic status. For families below the poverty level, that malleability only increases exponentially. Many of my kids, like Marvin, stayed in a number of different places all the time, some days at their grandmother's house, some days with their mothers, some days with an aunt. Living situations change day to day, not to mention year to year. What remains is a permeating sense of the temporary, the volatile, tempered with a profound desire to unpack and "stay" somewhere permanently.

The reasons that exacerbate this kind of family instability are many, but usually involve violence or poverty. Some kids stay with their grandmothers because their mothers work the 6 P.M. to 4 A.M. shift sewing underwear at Fruit of the Loom and don't want their children to be home alone all night. Some kids move to stay with their aunt because their mother's boyfriend is growing more abusive, and although she lacks the strength to part with him, she has the good sense to know that it is no place for a child. Some children stay with aunts or grandmothers simply because their mothers can't find work and the extra mouths are too many to feed right then. And still others stay with Grandma or Auntie because Mother has passed away or is having a bout with drugs, Dad is in prison, or Mom just couldn't take the burden of three little kids around the house all the time. This rootlessness is not a trivial complication in the life of an adolescent: It makes the otherwise difficult tasks of teaching adolescents responsibility almost superhuman.

Marvin's decision to "stay" with his aunt and uncle included all of the above. Marvin's aunt and uncle both had diabetes, and their son was mentally retarded, although just functional enough to hold down a job at the rice mill. Marvin's aunt was blind, his uncle permanently bedridden; after Marvin moved in, his uncle did not leave the bed other than to use the bathroom, and that with great struggle. A houseful of dependents, the three were having an especially hard time just keeping themselves alive. As a result, Marvin's mother decided that Marvin ought to move in to help them; so he did. Marvin would wake up at 5:00 every morning, in order to have half an hour of quiet time before he went to work. At 5:30 he began cooking breakfast for his aunt, uncle, and cousin, and packed a lunch for his cousin. By 6:00 he began work on household chores, cleaning and washing and folding clothes. After serving everyone breakfast, giving his cousin his lunch, and cleaning up the kitchen, he had ten minutes before his bus came for school. Each day after school, since no one in his house drove or shopped, he walked to the store to do whatever shopping was necessary for dinner and the next day's breakfast, or whatever other errands were needed. Then he returned home and began cooking dinner. After serving and cleaning up after dinner, and cleaning up any other part of the house that had become dissheveled since the morning, Marvin settled in to do whatever homework he had been assigned. I guessed that cleaning up was never a small task, as I had never visited Marvin's aunt's house on a day when his uncle did not have his friends seated around the bed, smoking, drinking, and eating. Any free time Marvin could muster was spent talking to Jerry, writing, or walking.

When Marvin first asked me to help him prepare for the ACT, his goal was to score a 30 (the ACT is scored on a scale of 36, where a 24 is roughly equivalent to 1000 on the SAT). The highest score at Greenville High the previous year had been a 23, scored by the salutatorian. As such, Marvin's goal was an ambitious one, but this ambition lasted only until he discovered that the highest score one could get was a 36; then his goal became, not surprisingly, a 36. For most Greenville students, the magic ACT number was 16—the minimum requirement to enter a four-year college in Mississippi without being subject to academic probation.

I asked Marvin why he was aiming so high. He replied, "I got to get at least a 30 so I can go to Alcorn State."

This befuddled me. Alcorn State is one of Mississippi's historically black colleges and, along with Mississippi Valley State University and Jackson State University, the most popular destination for college-bound students from Greenville. Valedictorians and disinterested students alike seem to end up at Alcorn State; its average ACT score is a 17 and its four-year graduation rate is lower than 25 percent. Little did Marvin know that Alcorn would probably take him sight unseen as a sophomore in high school with his present academic record. In some way this made the labor of our ACT preparation seem unnecessary.

When I asked him why he wanted to go to Alcorn, he responded, "Because my momma knows some people that went there, they say it's good, so that's where I'm going."

I decided to gradually introduce him to other colleges, explaining the differences in academic programs, student interests, and intellectual communities. Marvin simply wanted the best of all that he knew. On the ACT, when all that he knew was a 30, that was what he sought. From what he knew of college, Alcorn was the pinnacle. As his horizon broadened, so did his aspirations.

I gave Marvin information from colleges all over the country, gave him books that listed and compared all colleges, and even provided him with different sets of college rankings, merely to show him that colleges were a competitive business. My immediate desire was to cultivate Marvin's intellectual drive and direct him toward the nation's best schools. It was late one night when I was dropping Marvin off at his aunt's house that I began to think about Marvin's potential to attend a nationally renowned university. As I watched him glide up the stairs to his shotgun trailer, watched the screen door creak open and not close, I closed my eyes and thought about the sights he was seeing as he entered the house.

Like many nostalgic college graduates, I would have loved to see Marvin attend my alma mater, Yale. I pictured Marvin strolling out of my favorite classroom building from college, holding an obscure work of literature and joking with a fellow student about the previous night's reading. Then I remembered that even on a diverse campus like Yale's, English classes tended to be predominantly white. I could imagine Marvin with his old San Francisco 49ers Starter jacket on, which made me smile; but the loud red, black, and gold coat would be an obvious anomaly among the legion of navy J. Crew coats, black leather boots, charcoal scarves, and tortoise-rimmed glasses. I thought of Marvin's classmate inviting him for a sandwich at the café down the street. I knew that Marvin would not be able to afford an off-campus meal at Yale, let alone tuition, room, board, books, or a bus ticket to New Haven.

Each time a Greenville student had asked me where I went to college, they were often stunned, but the response was always similar: "Wow, you went to one of those rich schools." "Wow, your parents must be rich!" "You musta got a scholarship!" In Greenville, Yale was not seen as an unattainable academic achievement but as an impossible financial one. Competitive private colleges were not viewed as excellent so much as expensive. Despite many obvious hurdles, I believed Marvin capable not only of surviving but also of excelling on such a campus. Given his environment in Greenville, it was staggering how truly extraordinary he was.

I had spent so many afternoons in Marvin's house that his mother eventually came to claim me as her own son. My school photo sits on the wooden shelf next to the series of Marvin's and Floyd's photos. (Floyd is Marvin's only sibling; he was in the sixth grade and has a serious learning disability, a difficulty that passed the weight of all expectation and responsibility onto Marvin's shoulders.) I grew to love his mother and respect her deeply. From the moment she recognized Marvin's talent, she always demanded the very best from him. Each week when I passed by to play chess or chat with Marvin, I always brought a handful of books to trade with Marvin's mother. She was always ahead of me, providing reviews of the past week's selections and previews of the new books she had already begun.

Mostly Marvin and I played chess. The complexity, competition, and nobility of the game captivated him. I gave him a board early in the year that he carried with him tirelessly. In every idle moment he searched for a match: after school, before school, waiting for the bus, or sitting on the porch. His mental acuity translated effortlessly onto the chess board. His play was imaginative, sophisticated, and exacting, always searching for new techniques, always anxious to learn from someone better than him, always focusing intently on the million roads that diverged in the next five moves, deftly sorting and selecting among them. Marvin was the first student to beat me, and by the end of my second year, he won as often as I did. When I showed up to school at 7:30 in the morning he would already be sitting outside my door, sometimes two or three games along with Jerry. When I returned to my room after the last bell he would be sitting at my desk with the pieces already arranged, his first move already made. Those days when I didn't have a practice or a rehearsal to go to, Mr. Webster, the custodian, would come to my doorway and laugh, "I just about locked you folks in here again. It's going on seven o'clock. Y'all aint so much as shuffled a foot for three hours."

Marvin was an enigma. He had assumed none of the distaste for life that surrounded him; somehow he managed to develop from his rancid environment a perpetually hopeful and peaceful vision of his own world. Independently he found a way to nurture a profoundly inquisitive mind; he developed an extraordinary intelligence, honing it even as those skills became less and less popular—even to the point that they rubbed fiercely against the texture of his own existence. Considering the height of the obstacles faced by students like Marvin, we might assume that kids who would rather smoke pot than play chess would be as common as grass in Greenville, but they were not. What replaced them in unsung numbers were children who, disguised as misfits, were fighting for membership in a world where reason and wonder still reign.

In terms of the American family, William Alexander Percy was perhaps a hothouse flower that, raised with the right sunlight at the right temperature for the right amount of time, turned out exactly as one might hope. Marvin, on the other hand, was a wildflower that grew up through the cracks in the garage floor, never tended, never cultivated, but somehow willed toward full bloom. When a Greenvillian would shake his head and mutter that no one like Percy had come along since the Greenville schools integrated, I wanted to respond that in a culture of such privilege, I could not believe that white Greenville had produced only one Percy. In the forty years it had taken for integration to stumble into the Delta and stumble quickly back out, beleaguered by abject poverty, institutional negligence, omnipresent violence, and endless alienation,

I could not believe that we had been fortunate enough to produce one Marvin.

Marvin scored a 24 on his ACT, not as high as he would have hoped but high enough to incur a deluge of college mail. The stream of recruitment letters came from everywhere, offering scholarships and begging him to apply. They came from Morehouse, Vanderbilt, Emory, Harvard, Colgate, Princeton, and Yale. When Marvin told me, I was ecstatic and promised to go to work preparing letters of recommendation. Marvin was silent. His mother had already made a decision: He wasn't allowed to leave Mississippi. It was a battle I fought virulently before conceding, imploring her mother to see the possibilities afforded by a nationally renowned campus in a major city. I fought longest for Morehouse, Emory, and Vanderbilt, believing that their excellence and geographic proximity offered a fair compromise. In the end, Marvin agreed to spend his first year of college in Mississippi and his mom agreed that he could transfer after his first year if he chose to.

In late April 2001 Marvin decided he would attend Mississippi State University. The next day he was elected to the 2001 Greenville High School Hall of Fame.

I sometimes dreamed about what kind of homecoming Marvin might receive if he went on to be a great writer. I wondered if they would name a library after him or give him a tombstone with a stone soldier standing guard; or if Greenville might be proud enough to bury him somewhere within the iron gates of the graveyard where Percy's stone soldier already stands, in hopes that he might keep watch over them both.

THIRTEEN

By early October, when the routine of classroom chaos made it appear less chaotic, Coach Pierson repeated his offer to make me the assistant track coach. There were a number of variables that seemed to indicate it would be a bad choice to accept the position. Track season was the longest of any sport, beginning with indoor track in November and culminating in the outdoor state finals in the middle of May. It would demand practice every day of the week and full-day meets every Saturday. This meant starting to grade papers and plan lessons at 6 or 7 each night instead of 3:30. It also meant 6 A.M. Saturday departures and 10 P.M. returns, thereby eliminating one of my most productive workdays and one of the few moments during the week when I could breathe deeply and prepare for another immersion. In addition, I had already taken on the task of directing the senior play, which I had to select, audition, cast, rehearse, and produce during the three months that were the heart of the track season: December through March.

However, there were three very compelling reasons to take the position. First, it offered a wonderful opportunity to get to know students in a different setting. Second, students accorded coaches a certain reverence, a promotion that couldn't hurt my foundering attempts to tighten discipline in my room. Third—and most important—it would allow me to work with Chico.

Chico was one of the handful of people whom every individual in an eleven-hundred-person high school knew. I had watched Chico play football in the fall, and along with the legion of college scouts who sat by me in the stands, I was quite impressed. He played that Herculean combination of positions that is always reserved for the most outstanding athlete on a high school football field: kick returner, wide receiver, tailback, cornerback, and sometimes quarterback. The first time I saw Chico play—in fact, the first time I saw him touch the ball—he returned a kickoff 102 yards for a touchdown. That in itself was not as miraculous as the way he looked when he did it. From the moment Chico caught the ball and took his first two steps, the touchdown was inevitable. He moved so swiftly and easily that everyone else on the field appeared mired in some invisible viscosity. As his legs spun like a bicycle tire lifted from the ground, the rest of the players trudged after him like the cumbersome first turn of a gear.

Greenville High School went on to lose the game that night and most of its games that season, primarily because Chico could be in only one place at a time. He could not throw the ball to himself, nor could he hand it off to himself. Other teams devoted two or three players at a time to covering Chico. Unfortunately, the rest of our squad lacked the competence to take advantage of the triple coverage, for the farther Chico was from the ball, the less it moved.

Despite his prowess on the football field, track was always Chico's first sport. He had won the state championship in the 400-meter dash as a junior, winning every meet he entered in the last eighteen months. As football season petered to an ignominious close, Chico's spirits lifted as he became eager to unburden himself of his impossible responsibility on the field, and elated to devote himself to that which he did best, running. Chico had run the 400-meter in 48.8 seconds at the state finals the year before, nearly a second in front of the rest of the pack.

Coach Pierson told me that Chico's goal that year was to break the state record, almost a second and a half faster than his best time up to that point. Pierson formally pushed the job on me on a Thursday afternoon, leaning against the hood of his truck outside the school gymnasium. It was a Delta afternoon that gathered dust and heat so densely that they flowed across the flat land like a dirty liquid. Football practice was ending and the dirt lot between the field and the gym began to clutter with boys buried inside high shoulder pads. Pierson wanted to ask me for my decision here, where it could be influenced by the figure of Chico pacing restlessly in the background. As Pierson and I spoke, Chico circled us carefully, gathering clumps of boys as he moved.

Finally he approached Pierson, pretending that I wasn't there but asking questions that were obviously meant for my ears.

"Hey! D'you see dat number forty-two run back that kick-off return. That man bad! Couldn't nobody even touch him! You know he prob'ly the fastest man in the state."

Chico knew that Pierson had seen the touchdown because Pierson was the statistician for every game. In fact they had probably already spoken about it a number of times.

At this point Chico turned to me. "Hey, I suppose you never heard the legend of Chico. He a runner at Greenville High. Old Chinese secret say he the fastest black man on two legs. You know he's prob'ly gonna break the state record this year, although *Sports Illustrated* say he might could just take a million-dollar shoe contract and go pro instead."

"Yes," I responded, "I saw that runback, and I've heard about your state title last year. Coach tells me you're the hardest worker on the team."

"Yeah, but when you as good as me you don't too much need to train, I really just do that to help out the other guys, you know, peace, love, brotherhood, Wheaties boxes, all that kind of stuff. It's good for the school image."

Chico started to walk away, blessed with a comedian's sense of timing. On the way, he stopped, turned to Coach Pierson, and placed his ear up against the side of Pierson's massive belly as he tapped the top of it. Before Pierson could swat him, Chico ducked his head and skidded away like a hyena, remarking over his shoulder, "Yep, she's coming along just fine, ought to be any day now. Don't forget that breathing I showed you!"

As a college athlete, I had spent a good deal of time around athletes of great promise and came to know the arrogance that seems inextricably bound to their abilities. But Chico was quite different. His athletic abilities caught my attention, but the eccentricities of his personality held that attention long enough to make me his coach.

Academics were a different story for Chico. The quickness of his wit suggested that his academic failings were due more to apathy than to incompetence. The combination of his exalted status, his shrewd but endearing smile, and his general evasiveness seemed to confirm that his propensity was for clowning with teachers who tolerated it (or didn't know how not to tolerate it), and withdrawing from teachers who looked for opportunities to put disruptive students in their place. Coach Pierson constantly interrogated Chico about his grades, and had paid twice for Chico to attend summer school, both times without repayment from Chico's family.

Chico lived alone with his mother, although Chico's cousin became a frequent visitor after his wife put him out. I saw Chico's cousin on the news before I ever knew he was related to Chico—he had driven his car through the side of his wife's house after a tumultuous fight. The situation only deteriorated. Some weeks later Chico confided that his cousin had been forcing his sixteen-year-old-daughter Toya to have sex with him for the past two years. Chico asked me to wait twenty-four hours before notifying any authorities. The next morning Toya did not come to school; she and her mother had disappeared in the middle of the night. By the time school let out, Chico's cousin had already set out looking for them. I knew only that they had gone somewhere in Florida, and that everyone prayed the cousin never found them.

Our first track meet that spring was at home. It was a March Saturday when the Mississippi Delta heat was held in abeyance just enough to make it a pleasant day for spectators to meander around the track. Due to the magnetic pull of Chico's personality and his athletic prowess, we had assembled quite a capable and diversely talented team. Ken Cooks was our sprinter who would run the 100-meter and 200-meter. Chico had met him at a barbecue, and when the boy challenged Chico to a race in the street and Ken won, Chico made him come out for track. Reginald "Hawk" Carter would run the 800-meter and the mile; Derrick Dorsey, a junior who had been Chico's protégé on the football team, would long-jump, triple jump, and run the 400-meter. Chico would run only the 400-meter, and together these four would run all three of our relays. The first day was one of great promise: Ken Cooks won the 100-meter and finished second in the 200-meter, Derrick won the long jump, Reginald won the 800-meter and finished third in the mile, and Chico won the 400-meter by twenty-five meters.

The afternoon light settled into the dirt, and evening pulled itself over the Delta like a porous gray curtain leaking light in shards as it shifted in the breeze. Nonetheless, the crowd gathered, milled, crossed and uncrossed their arms, but did not leave. The two early relays had been exciting; we had won the 4 × 200-meter and finished second in the 4 × 100-meter, both tight races. As the girls lined up for the final event of the day, the 4 × 400-meter relay, spectators grew alert, seeking out good seats, open sections of fence, sight lines to the finish. In the infield it was the same: Athletes, coaches, officials all swirled around the finish tent like mosquitoes beneath a street lamp. The bleachers and sitting areas where the teams had laid out all of their belongings for the day were now deserted. Everyone had migrated to the center of the track where they clustered in groups, offering support, conjecture, intimidation.

In high school track-and-field, the 4 × 400-meter relay is the crown jewel of the track meet. The 100-meter dash retains a special aura, as the simplest and most elevated title in all of sports—the fight to be the fastest runner. But the 100-meter expires before it begins, a wisp of a race that leaves one wondering how much heart was really spent, and how much more one could have given for such a short distance. The 4 × 400 is a team effort of the greatest magnitude. The final event of the day, it calls on each team's four best athletes, who have already been competing in other events for ten painstaking hours. It asks them not so much to tap the strength in their legs as is it does to call up what remains of the stamina in their hearts. For someone who has never run the 400-meter, some describe it as the longest sustainable sprint. Where the 100-meter demands hitting top speed as quickly as possible, the 400-meter demands maintaining top speed for as long as possible. To inexperienced runners this amounts to a fast jog with a kick at the end, but to those who run it well, it is the art of pouring out a full glass of water over exactly forty-eight seconds, making sure that one doesn't expend the water before the time is up, and sure that one does not leave anything left in the glass.

The whole track had stopped when Chico ran the individual 400-meter earlier in the day. He did it perfectly, long thin legs cycling in a stride that matched speed with precision, strength with grace. He modulated ever so carefully the four 100-meter segments of the track: lente, allegro, allegro, lente. As dusk encroached, people waited not just to see the 4 × 400-meter relay but also to see Chico run again, to prove that it was not the uneven contours of memory that painted their exalted picture of him circling the track with such majesty.

We were in second place going into the fourth and final leg of the relay. This was not so discouraging as the fact that when Chico finally got the baton, we were in second place by nearly one hundred meters. The leader was already rounding the far corner and turning down the straightaway by the time Chico left the starting line. I was convinced that the race was over, and gave Chico a perfunctory clap as he sped by me into the curve. Then I turned my back on him and began walking toward the finish line. Two steps along the way I saw Derrick staring straight at me, a ridiculous smile spread across his face.

"You don't think he gonna do it. You walking away. Mannn, you just don't know. He gonna reel that boy in like he standing still. You think that boy playing, you never seen him run befo'. Chico don't lose."

"I know Chico doesn't lose on his own, but in a relay, when he's a hundred meters behind, there ain't even much *Chico* can do in that situation."

"Bet!" Derrick shouted. "You watch! You watch and see why he call himself the fastest black man on two legs." Then Derrick pointed over my shoulder and yelled, "Man, that boy wide open!" Derrick began hopping and I turned to follow his excitement. Chico had rounded the curve and was into the first straightaway; the boy in front of him was almost out of the straightaway and into the second curve, still a good seventy-five meters ahead. As Derrick bounced across the infield, waving his hands and smiling irrepressibly, the other boys flocked toward him, pulled not so much by him as by the magic that he already realized. I watched Chico swallow the straightaway in what seemed like six strides. Before I could enjoy the beauty of his wide-open gait, he was already into the curve and the boy ahead of him not yet out of it. I felt myself smile so widely that I was embarrassed a second later when I saw another coach looking at me. As the face of the boy in the lead contorted, Chico's relaxed; as the leader's stride tired and wobbled, Chico's strengthened and elongated. The boy survived the last curve and turned down the final stretch, his hands reaching out with the despair of a man falling backward. Fifty meters from the finish line, Chico, still accelerating, blew past him.

Derrick flew by me, turning as he bounced, "What I tell you? Wide open! Man, that boy bad! That man pulled in buddy from a hundred meters back. Ain't nobody never seen that happen in Greenville before."

Standing beside me was the local DJ who had been announcing the event. A gray-bearded portly fellow, he had been a community landmark as a high school sports commentator for over twenty years. He looked at me with his mouth open, contemplating something.

"I believe he's right," he said. "I ain't never seen nothing like it."

Newspaper reporters scribbled, coaches lifted their hats and smoothed their balding heads, athletes from other teams laughed and cursed at the same time, all calling Chico by name.

"D'you see Chico, man, that nigga wide open!"

"They might as well give that boy the state title right now."

"I'm sho' glad I don't run no four-hundred, I'd pack up my bags and take up the pole vault or some shit. Ain't no sense in even runnin' that event right dere. Ain't nobody gonna catch that boy."

Across the tent I caught Coach Pierson's eye. He smiled and shook his head, lifting his hat to scratch the side of his head. He motioned me over with his other hand. When I stopped and stood beside him he did not speak, but proffered his stopwatch. He always timed the splits for each leg of the relay; the clock read 47.79. Before I could respond, I felt a head burrowing into the narrow space between our bodies, "What we got?"

It was Chico. Still holding the baton, a legion of fans behind him, he wanted to see what his time was. Only his head visible, I read him the time. Although it was unofficial and relay times tended to be faster than regular 400-meter times, he looked up at me unmoved. "Dat's what I figured, I slowed down there at the end, I knew that boy didn't have nothing. That ain't a bad first race, though."

I looked at the watch, and when I looked back to Chico, he was gone. Pierson tilted his head back and laughed full-voiced, part cackle, part disbelief.

Chico won every race he entered, and despite the loss of Derrick to a broken ankle, incurred in a game of pickup basketball, the rest of our team fared quite well that season. We flew through the qualifying rounds for the state meet, medaling in the 100-meter, 200-meter, 400-meter, 800-meter, 1600-meter, and all three relays at the final north state qualifying meet. In the meantime, Coach Pierson and I were occupied with the task of helping Chico decide on his next step. Despite the magnitude of his athletic talent, his horizon was cluttered with a number of barriers, obstacles that seemed to encroach every day. Scholarship offers poured in from schools as formidable as UCLA and Mississippi State and as unknown as Hinds Community College. All of them either knew Chico's times or had seen him run, so their first question was always the same: "What do his grades look like?"

There are two stipulations for NCAA eligibility: As an incoming freshman, a student must have a 2.5 GPA and a 17 on the ACT—the equivalent of a combined 700 on the SAT. Chico's GPA was well below a 2.5 and he had already taken the ACT once and had scored 14. One Tuesday night Pierson and I decided to take Chico out for dinner after practice to discuss his options for the future.

Coach Pierson had a particular seafood place where he liked to eat, one of the few restaurants in Greenville where servers took the orders. Chico was quiet and made little eye contact as we waited to order. He studied the menu and the surroundings with self-conscious fascination.

"Where do we go to order at?" he asked.

Pierson had taken Chico out to eat at cafeterias before, but he knew that Chico had never eaten in a restaurant with menus and a waitress. "Don't you worry about it, man, they gonna come over to us and ask us what we want, so you get it figured out." Chico ordered a hamburger, I ordered the fried catfish, and Pierson ordered crawfish tails—or crawdad tails, as he called them. After the waitress departed, we sat in silence. Chico studied the floor beneath his feet, pushing the cap of the hot sauce around with his shoe.

Coach Pierson began, "Let's talk, man. D'you talk to Ms. Crockett today?"

"Yeah, she say she gonna check on the correspondence thing tomorrah."

Slightly confused, I interrupted, "What correspondence thing?"

Coach Pierson breathed deeply, picked up his fork and tapped it on the side of the table, then exhaled loudly, "Well, Coach, we got us a little problem. Come to find out yesterday that ol' Chico here ain't fixing to walk across that stage in May."

"What do you mean, he's not going to graduate? I thought you were passing everything."

Chico still didn't look up; Pierson answered for him.

"Well it's not that exactly, supposably we still passing everything this semester, Chico, ain't that right?" Pierson, a native Mississippian, spoke with a country drawl that he had blended with the speech patterns of our students, creating a comfortable hybrid of Mississippi dialects. Chico nodded listlessly.

Pierson continued, "The problem is, Momma goes in to check on Chico's grades yesterday and come to find out Chico's one credit short. Don't quite know where it went to or how we miscounted, but Chico is one credit short, and it's already late March and ain't a whole lot we can do about it. So right now Ms. Crockett's trying to get him hooked up with a correspondence credit through some high-school-in-a-mailbox program where you can do work and send it in to some national office where they give you that one credit you need. But we still don't know if that can happen all quick enough for Chico to flip the tassel and take the photo in the cap and gown."

I turned to Chico, "Did you get your new ACT scores back yet?"

Chico decided to lean over and pick up the hot-sauce cap, his head disappearing under the table.

"Well, Coach," Pierson continued, " that's not the best of the news either. Tell him what you got, Kendrix." Pierson was the only one who ever called Chico by his real name.

The sound he made was again barely audible and I had to ask him to repeat it.

"Fifteen," Chico answered. "That place was too crowded, man. They had you sitting at these little tiny desks with four or five people on either side of you, no air-conditioning, I fell asleep for part of it. And on the day of a track meet too. Ain't no way."

"Chico, why didn't you come in to see me for help?" I asked him. "I gave you the review book and you never brought it back. You knew when I was hosting review sessions, all you had to do was stop by. Did you ever even take those practice tests I gave you?"

"I looked at 'em some. My uncle be trying to help me out with that math part, but it didn't never come out right. He say those tests don't measure nothing noway."

"So what does that mean for Mississippi State?" I asked. "Are they still interested?"

"Oh yeah, they're still interested," Pierson remarked. "It's just the NCAA that ain't interested—no seventeen, no run. He might could go there anyway and stay on academic probation for a year and then start running, but they won't accept him if he don't have a high school diploma."

"Chico, what do you think?" I asked.

"I seen those guys' times at Mississippi State, I can take them boys. They fastest guy run a 46.4 and he a senior. You give me one year of college training, I be running 45s. I was looking in that track magazine Coach got, the fastest time in the country for high school right now is a 47.2. Man, I just about ran that on that relay when I pulled that boy in, and that wasn't even with competition. I jes' need some competition, then I can take any of dem folks."

"I think you're right, Chico," I responded, "but we still gotta decide what we're going to do about next year."

"Maybe I should just go pro, like Kevin Garnett or sump'n, forget college."

"Well," Pierson began, "that's a little tougher to do in track-and-field. Folks aren't quite beating down the door to offer a 400-meter runner a multimillion-dollar contract. Only way to get there is through college athletics."

"Well, what are my choices? I ain't got no choices really."

I could see Pierson began to feel guilty about just how bleak a picture he had painted.

"Well, that's not true exactly," He said. "We know you can go to Hinds Community College for two years and then transfer to a four-year college. There might be a few colleges that will take you without a high school diploma on some sort of probation, maybe Grambling or University of Arkansas at Pine Bluff. We just gotta go on down to state and put on our best show and see what comes up. How's that sound?"

Chico nodded his head, looking at the ground again. Then he picked his head up and tossed Coach Pierson one of the breath mints he had pilfered from the entrance of the restaurant.

"Little something for ya," he said. "You know you gonna have some stanky breath after eating all those crawdad butts. Whatever a crawdad is."

* * *

On the May morning of the state track meet in Jackson, summer crept up on the retreating borders of spring like an overwhelming army, pushing its temperateness back into fading memory. By 8 A.M. when our bus stopped in a flurry of its own dust at the track, summer had already carried the day, with a rising heat sweating from the grass and the rocks and the dirt. Athletes covered their heads with shirts, seeking shelter under umbrellas and bleachers and the dripping of orange water jugs.

The Mississippi High School State Championship Track Meet is a sight to behold. In the smaller-school classifications there is a predominance of white athletes, representing the private white academies and the towns small enough to retain public schools with white majorities or politically resourceful enough to engineer district lines to create them. As one ventures into the middle-size classifications, the racial makeup equalizes rapidly: a scattering of middle-size high schools that have succeeded in the integration experiment, or are balancing precariously somewhere on the curve between integration and resegregation. However, by the time the largest classification, 5A, roughly one thousand students and over, takes the track, the white athlete is a rarity, appearing only sporadically in the pole vault or a distance event. Because the larger schools outweigh the smaller ones in numbers as well as athletic prowess, the event is very much the property of the black community of Mississippi. The celebration resonates with the energy of a barbecue and the reverence of a church outing. The air swells and breaks with laughter, while the heat is steadily brushed away by swaying programs and private talk of sport past and present. Because the biggest schools tend to have the fastest and the strongest athletes in the state, even the predominantly white news channels and community leaders turn an eye to track the stories of the day.

Our team had only six athletes who qualified for the state meet through success in the district and regional rounds. Derrick had nursed his foot back to health in time to join the relay team together with Ken Cooks, Reginald, and Chico. Other than that we brought only a triple jumper, Fred, and our discus thrower, Dexter. The possibility of competing for the overall state title looked doubtful because we didn't have enough athletes in enough events to compile team points. As more and more athletes were eliminated during the qualifying rounds, however, our outlook improved. Early in the season, other teams had beaten us by doing moderately well in many different events because there were many events for which we did not enter a single athlete, but we frequently won the events we did enter. Now that all the teams retained only a select number of athletes participating in a select number of events, our chances improved greatly.

Chico turned heads wherever he walked. The story of the comeback in Greenville and his second consecutive season without a defeat in the 400-meter was now well known in every 5A high school in Mississippi. In a season where many events had been hotly contested, Chico was already the king of the 400. Before the meet began he was announced over the PA system as a returning state champion. Applause was only sporadic but the crowd quieted at the announcement. Chico ducked his head under the bleachers and pretended to be fixing his shoes.

The beginning of the meet was awkward and self-conscious, like the first hours of a high school dance. It was not until midday that the event seemed to build upon its own momentum and hasten toward resolution. By the time Chico was ready to run the 400-meter open, we had already finished second in the 100-meter and the 200-meter and third in the triple jump. This group of 400-meter runners stayed with Chico longer than any other I had yet seen, but none of them was ever a threat. Their bodies, more muscular and powerful than Chico's, constricted under their own force, labored in spite of themselves. By the time Chico entered the second curve, he was all alone. I stood on the finish line, screaming and motioning to him as fervently as I could. Chico always slowed down for the last forty meters because, as he put it, "Ain't nobody coming." If somehow through my unintelligible fits I could inspire him to run the last forty meters like the first forty, he could capture the record he was chasing.

When he crossed the finish line, the whole crowd was on its feet, more in awe than in celebration. As I caught my breath I checked my stopwatch. It read 47.15—nearly half a second faster than the state record—but I knew hand times were always a little fast. Before I could locate him, Chico was standing beside me; his breath already regained, he wanted to see the watch. I showed him. "Dat's about what I figured," he said, and smiled. "I slowed down the last ten."

While we waited in silence for the official announcement, teammates paraded over with boundless enthusiasm. Adversaries stood patiently by, waiting out the commotion for a chance to offer Chico heartfelt congratulations. Chico always knew where these people were and sought them out. His disposition was always the same before and after the race: calm, polite, comedic, but slightly reserved.

The PA system sounded and silence fell over the stadium.

"The winner of the 400 meter dash, setting a new 5A state record, Kendrix Washington from Greenville High School finishing in a time of 47.55. Oh my Lord, folks, setting a new 5A state record and only one one-hundredth of a second off of the overall state title of 47.54! A new 5A state record for Kendrix Washington, 47.55—only one one-hundredth of a second off of the overall state title of 47.54."

The jumping and hugging that engulfed Chico resumed, and I managed to penetrate it far enough to give Chico a hug. "Man, one one-hundredth of a second," he grimaced, "I shoulda had that."

"But you set the 5A record, you did it," I said.

"Yeah, but one one-hundredth . . . man."

I released Chico, and the swarm of boys that closed quickly around him ushered him off.

As the daylight shifted and the sun began its procession toward the horizon, Reginald claimed the gold medal in the 800-meter run and our relay team claimed gold in the 4 × 200-meter relay. In 5A, our division, Pearl High School already held an insurmountable thirty-point lead, but heading into the 4 × 400-meter relay, the last event, we found ourselves tied for second place. A win in the 400-meter relay would guarantee us the second-place trophy.

Derrick, Ken, and Reginald ran their legs of the race stoically but cautiously, as they knew that was all Chico required of them. Gone was the reckless stamina of races past, replaced with a tenacious and calculating focus—each handoff must be clean even if it meant wasting the extra second to look back over your shoulder for the baton. Chico didn't need a lead: A race we were still in was a race Chico could win.

When Chico received the baton trailing by only twenty-five meters, our team burst into celebration. The other athletes and spectators were confused at first, but quickly understood our elation when Chico rocketed past the leader before the hapless runner had made it into the heart of the first straightaway.

Day finally succumbed to darkness with our four boys arm in arm atop the modest wooden award stand. We managed to capture the title of state runner-up, the highest team athletic honors Greenville High School had achieved in any sport in the 1990s.

Although Pearl took home the state title, an undeniable aura of victory emanated from our team. As the other teams filed out of the stadium, they watched our boys with wistful eyes. As spectators and parents gathered their debris and left the stands, the stories of the boys from Greenville High decorated the dusk settling among the silent cars. And when the meet was done, it was our boys who were cornered by the men who had spent the day conspicuously consulting their watches, rubbing their chins, and scribbling furtive notes. True to Coach Pierson's prediction, scouts had come from all over the South, and the sum of each of their careful calculations pointed them toward one runner: Chico.

When I saw the nest of recruiters cornering Coach Pierson at the gate, Chico and the relay team were still atop the awards stand. Soon after I observed the scouts, I could see that the boys noticed them as well. All four of their heads turned toward Pierson and the men who stood anxiously around him in the tableau common to the press ensnaring a celebrity. As the crowd turned to pack up their gear and head for home, the boys stepped down from the podium. Ken and Reginald hurried anxiously toward the college recruiters and Derrick began to follow ambivalently, noticing that Chico was standing firmly in place.

I waved Derrick along. "Go ahead on, we'll be over in a minute."

Derrick trotted off and Chico and I locked eyes. He showed no sign of moving, so I walked over to him. Even when I stood in front of him he looked past me. It was the first time I had ever seen him look nervous.

"You call the shots, man," I said. "You're the one they're here to see."

Chico paused for a moment and looked at the finish line, then turned to follow his eyes all the way around the track. "One one-hundredth of a second. Damn, I wanted that state record, it was those last ten yards, I knew I slowed down those last ten yards. If I had just pushed a little harder . . ."

"You got the Five-A record anyway, that's the best one to have."

"Yeah, but I wanted it all though."

"I know, I wanted it for you. What do you want to do about the ol' boys over here?"

Chico looked at the bleachers, squalid remnants of the celebration that was.

"I don't want to talk to any of them," he said. "I just don't. None of them."

"Whatever you say, Chico. Today's your day."

"Yeah, I guess this one's mine, huh?" Then after a pause, he looked back toward the bleachers. "I'm going to go get my stuff."

I took the job of keeping the recruiters away from Chico very seriously. If he really didn't want to talk to them, that was one service I could provide. I walked over to Pierson and the recruiters as Reginald, Ken, and Derrick were walking away toward the bus.

As I arrived, the silence broke with the coach from Grambling saying, "There just ain't nothing we can do with those grades, maybe if you send him to junior college for a year or two and he pulls up the ACT."

"Yeah, I know," added the coach from Mississippi State, "we'd love to have all of 'em come, especially Chico. I think we'd all be fighting over him if the grades were there, or even the diploma or the ACT, but there's just not too much we can do."

"Where is he? It'd still be nice to talk to him," the LSU coach said.

"He's already gone to the bus," I said, breaking in. "He's tired and a little overstimulated. You can call Coach Pierson at school if you need information."

The coaches looked at me a little surprised, obviously not used to dealing with athletes who weren't eager to visit with a Division-I coach. After a long silence one of them said okay and handed Coach Pierson his card. Soon the others did the same, shook hands, and departed.

Only one coach remained, the one from Hinds Community College. He had lingered silently at the periphery of the group while the other coaches fired their questions, waiting patiently for them to exhaust their inquiries and depart, knowing their labor would be in vain. Coach Pierson and the coach from Hinds stared silently at each other like the last two kids left without dancing partners. They understood that fate had made this decision, and there was no sense in pretending otherwise.

"Whacha say you just give me a call next week, we'll get it worked out. I know the boys are tired. You don't need my card, you know the number."

"Yeah," Pierson exhaled, "I know the number. Take care, Sammy."

The Hinds coach departed and Pierson and I were left alone. He fanned the stack of cards across the palm of his open hand, "Don't know what the hell I got these things for, Coach, you want 'em?"

"Nah, I don't want 'em."

"You know I did everything I could to keep this from turning out like this. It shouldn't have turned out like this. Not this one."

When I got back to the bus, Chico was already nestled into his seat, staring out the window. A number of the girls from our track team huddled around him, talking to him and about him as he studied the backs of the bleachers and the broken glimpses of the track that crept through the spaces between the flights. His head was high and he was still smiling. I tried to muster a smile when I boarded the bus and plopped down into the seat directly behind Pierson, who was at the wheel.

Chico knew what awaited and he wanted none of it; this was his moment and he wasn't about to give it up. He did not creep to the edge of the fence and peek into the future as I had. For Chico the future was coming soon enough. Graduation was only ten days away and he was still not eligible for a diploma.

A week before graduation, Chico was named the Mississippi Gatorade High School Athlete of the Year, and we managed to persuade the counselors that his enrollment in the correspondence course made it appropriate for him to march with his classmates from the class of 1998 at graduation, though he would not actually receive the diploma until he finished the correspondence course in early July. Chico—along with Ken, Reginald, Fred, and Dexter— enrolled at Hinds Community College in the fall.

Chico reshaped his vision for his own future so that it could include Hinds without abandoning the things he had once dreamed of. He assured me that his plan was to run for two years at Hinds, bring his time down to a 45, and then head off to UCLA or whomever offered him the best deal. Early in his tenure he appeared to be on track to achieve those goals. Reports from both the coach at Hinds and Chico himself indicated that he was working diligently, distinguishing himself as someone with sizable talent and an enviable work ethic. He medaled in the first three races he entered, then went on to win four consecutive events after that. His time had not dropped into the 46s yet, but he had run consistent 47s, good enough to rank him in the top ten of the junior college national rankings, thereby launching himself into contention for the title of fastest 400-meter man on the junior college circuit.

It was the following March when Coach Pierson received the phone call telling him that Chico was in jail. He was riding with another boy from Hinds when they got pulled over, and the police found two ounces of pot under the seat. Chico was arrested for possession of marijuana and spent the night in jail while he waited for someone to bail him out. He claimed only halfheartedly to know nothing about where the pot came from, but the coach admitted that he had already caught Chico smoking pot once in the parking lot and had issued him a warning. Chico was suspended from competition for two weeks and placed on probationary status by the athletic department. He missed two important races in the interim, but he still retained a ranking in the top ten due to his stellar performances early in the season—good enough to earn him a bid to the junior college track-and-field national finals. Pierson and I had wanted to travel to Nashville to watch him compete at the nationals, but we had a meet of our own that weekend. Chico finished third with a time only slightly faster than the time he had run at the Mississippi state meet a year before. Two important meets remained before the year was out, two more chances for Chico to establish himself as the front-runner heading into next season, but five days after the nationals, Chico was caught with marijuana by the campus police, and he was kicked off the team. In junior colleges, a student athlete is required to go to the closest junior college that offers his sport in order to avoid recruitment among competing junior colleges. As a result, Chico could not transfer to another junior college to run for another team. He had neither taken the ACT again nor shown the academic promise at Hinds that might make him eligible for an early transfer to a four-year institution.

If you watch closely enough, you can see the trajectory of something dying long before the moment when we mourn its loss. Like a football hurled deep downfield, even in the process of its rising we can sense the beginning of the fall. I knew that Chico's dream was over long before the phone call from Hinds; I saw it on his face earlier in the fall semester.

Greenville High School had wanted to host a special ceremony to award Chico his Gatorade High School Athlete of the Year plaque because the award had been given too late in the previous school year to organize any formal presentation. The athletic director decided to do it during halftime of an important home football game.

The score at halftime was 21–12, with Greenville High trailing. Derrick, now the eminent star, had scored both Greenville High touchdowns, but the kicker had missed both extra points. One of Derrick's touchdowns had been a punt return reminiscent of the first touchdown I had seen Chico score the year before. Derrick had appropriated Chico's charisma and legend, playing many of the same positions, always hovering somewhere around the ball, trying in vain to convince the other team that in the end the ball was not certain to come his way. At the concession stand and in the bleachers, all the talk was about Derrick. The stadium teemed with young boys weaving envy and worship into the bright tapestry of Derrick's indomitable ability, girls retelling jokes of his and standing on tiptoe to catch his eye as he took a rare rest on the sideline, grown men remarking with casual awe about his fine potential—sure that he was one of the finest to come along in years—and comparing him to the greats of their own bygone days.

I did not see Chico in the stands until they called him onto the field at halftime. He wore a red baseball cap with an "H" in the middle, apparently for Hinds. Standing at the fifty-yard line without football pads on, he looked fragile and suspect, as if Greenville High had invited home the Athlete of the Year from 1958 rather than 1998, and that was just the sort of welcome he received when he was introduced. The students in the stands seemed not to know him, or not to claim him. Few even turned their attention to the field as the ceremony progressed. Parents and spectators were irritated that the regular halftime extravaganza—the marching band—was not taking the field. Chico received his plaque to a scattering of perfunctory applause, the microphone clicked and huffed and turned off in the hands of the athletic director, and, accompanied by the silence that hovered above the empty grass, Chico walked swiftly from the field.

I caught his eye as he was passing under the bleachers, and waved him up to sit with me. Seconds later he slid furtively into the seat next to me, removing the red Hinds hat, in case it might lead someone to recognize him as the gentleman who had been perched awkwardly at midfield just minutes ago. I offered him congratulations on his award and asked him how things were going at Hinds.

"It's going all right so far," he said. "We're training pretty hard."

"What do you think of the rest of the team, the coach and all?"

"The coach is all right, he don't do that much. And I'm the fastest middle-distance guy they got, ain't nobody to push me in training or nothing. I had better training here with Derrick."

"Yeah, how about Derrick, he seems to be doing pretty well, huh? Scout from Mississippi State's here to see him play tonight."

"Yeah, I saw that clown, same dude came to see me play last year. He gonna leave right after he ask Derrick how his grades look. I see Derrick playing my position too. That's awright tho', it's all good, we probably be sharing a room down at Hinds next year."

"You gonna stay for the second half of the game?"

"Naw, I'm fixing to bounce, ain't nothing to see here, they just psyching all these kids' heads up, make 'em believe they something. They ain't. None of these kids ain't going nowhere. Jus' wouldn't be no fun to tell 'em that now. Wouldn't be no point to Derrick gettin' all hyped up and playing if he knew it ain't gonna amount to nothing."

"Yeah, we're trying to get Derrick's credits together right now, he's in more trouble than you were."

"It don't matter what his grades is, he still think he living it. People worshiping him for what they think he gonna do, even when they know he ain't gonna do it. Then when he don't, they pretend they ain't never seen 'im befo'. Man, Coach, you jes' don't know, when you down there, you think you *it*! All these folks coming to watch you play, folks clearing out in the hallways when you walk by, women you don't even know telling their daughters to go talk to you, grown men from big colleges showing up and kissing your butt and offering you full scholarships and money and everything else. Don't nothing else matter. You *it*! Look, you see those two little chickenheaded girls leaning over the railing, the ones been trying to holler at Derrick all night."

I recognized the two girls from the hallway outside my room, where they tended always to carry the attention or the hand of at least one boy.

"Coach, you jes' don't know how many times those two tried to get me to hit that last year. I'm talking about straight-up telling me, 'Chico, I'm ready whenever you want me.' Tonight, those girls

walk right by me, didn't even speak. Parents—even teachers—
done me the same way all night! 'Cause to see me, it make this all
fall down. To see me wearing this Hinds hat instead of some UCLA
hat, driving a big 4Runner, that makes dem tickets they just paid
good money for a damn waste. It make all of these folk talking
crazy about all this potential a whole lot of bullshit." He paused
for a long moment. "I'm sorry, Coach, I didn't mean no offense by
the cursing."

"That's all right, Chico."

Chico gave me his phone number and asked me to call. I was
taken aback at such a forceful invitation to friendship, and saddened
by the obvious loneliness it denoted. He offered no explanation, but
handed me the piece of paper with his phone number on it.

We embraced and I watched him walk through the crowd
and out to the parking lot by himself. As he crossed the edge of the
field, the Greenville Hornets burst out of the gymnasium to take
the field for the second half. Chico stopped to watch them storm
by. I saw him open his mouth in a bark and noticed Derrick turn
toward the sound of his own name. Derrick was at the head of the
sea of shoulder pads that was throbbing toward the field, and he
managed only a glance to look for the voice that called him, and
then returned to his boisterous run toward the field. Derrick
seemed not to notice Chico, or not to recognize him. Chico turned
to leave as the rest of the team stampeded by. He understood the
haze in which Derrick reveled; he saw the way Derrick wrapped
himself so tightly in the promise of the future that he was able to
obscure any view of the catastrophic present.

I stayed in the stands for the second half, and for many halves
afterward. But as I watched that day, I could think only of Chico.
Each year we find the strength to build a new icon out of the remnants
of the old, and each year we believe more fiercely than ever that this
one will navigate the storms of a disinterested world and land safely
somewhere on the other side. Perhaps we have no other choice.

FOURTEEN

M ario was one of those high school boys who spends much of his energy trying to convince his peers that he is no longer a boy. Having not yet reached his growth spurt, he was shorter than most of the girls in the class. Although there were only eighteen students in his second-block class, he made a habit of sitting by himself all the way on the far side of the room, midway down the last row, pressed against the chalkboard. His choice not to sit all the way in the far corner, which would have been the most obvious sign of rebellion, indicated he didn't want to sever all ties with the rest of us; he wanted to be a part of the class, but wished to do so on his own terms—a tepid rejection, more playful than hurtful. I saw no harm in that, and from that day forward allowed it.

I first learned to recognize Mario's handwriting when it emerged as the forensic match to the "DON'T FUCK WIT COLOMBO" graffiti that proliferated all over my room. I had been conducting a private investigation for some weeks when I recognized the compact small letters, stylized with slightly crooked edges that would have been a suitable font for a children's story about a haunted house. Once my investigation had yielded the chief suspect, I confirmed my suspicion by dropping in on Mario unexpectedly during class to see what scribbles he was making on his notebook. If he was not making elaborate and quite sophisticated drawings of warriors and cars, his doodling always involved some contortion of the word "Colombo." When I found the same word graffittied on Mario's desk, first in pencil, then in pen, and then in permanent marker, the match was complete.

Mario was an insightful young man. Although his attention waxed and waned, when he made contributions to group discussions they were succinct and trenchant—then he'd drift back to Colombo and would not be heard from, perhaps for the rest of the class.

It was late one weeknight when I was grading papers and contemplating a course of action for the Colombo vandal. I knew that Colombo was an offshoot of the Vicelords. It was a rather small group of guys who lived off Colombo Street and liked to go cruising together and smoke a lot of marijuana. Sometimes they carried guns and occasionally got caught in a knife fight or drive-by. Like most gang members in the school, Mario seemed altogether too intelligent, too rational, too decent to be deeply connected to Colombo. The chances were good that he had an older cousin or even a next-door neighbor who was a member, and he flashed the guy's name the way any vulnerable child flashes the name of his father or his big brother, a sort of oversized jacket to protect himself from the night's shivers and silent darkness.

As I thought of him, I searched for Mario's assignment and read it. It was outstanding—I could not hold back a smile and laughed out loud. The next day I read Mario's essay in front of the class, lauding its successes and holding it up as a model to be emulated by other students. His wiry lips parted just far enough to reveal a smile, and to reveal that he was fighting hard to keep it from spreading any farther than it already had.

I continued to praise Mario's writing when it merited it, which turned out to be quite often, and he continued to work more and more diligently on each writing assignment. Gradually his enthusiasm began to spread to other aspects of the class. Some weeks later I received a rather mediocre pile of papers, and nestled at the bottom was Mario's truly inspired work. He had forgone two of the other assignments in class that day to work on his composition, and the result was a piece of writing that was more sophisticated, thoughtful, and poetic than any I had seen in my two months as a high school teacher.

Eager to congratulate him, and aware of what a pleasant effect my reinforcement was having on him, the next day after class I spared no honesty in telling Mario that it was the most poignant piece of writing I had read at Greenville High School. He glowed when I handed him his paper, and chuckled mischievously. I knew that was how Mario saw it: While the rest of the students toiled and ignored him, he, the aloof thug, had labored his way to the top of the class, and none of them knew it. They presumed him to be the illiterate, antagonistic roughneck that most of his friends were, but the joke was on them.

By midterm Mario's grade had climbed from a low D to a low B. When midterm report cards came out Mario was silent, but smiling. He did not make a peep in class, and when I passed by he was not drawing or scribbling, but simply twisting his pencil in his hand and contemplating something I could not decipher. Class ended and his classmates filed out. Mario loitered long enough to make sure that he was the last one in the room, but not long enough for anyone to assume that he was actually waiting to talk to me. He pushed his report card toward me. There was the B in my class, a C in algebra II, and a C in carpentry. I was unimpressed, until I looked back at his first quarter grades and noticed that my D was his highest grade for the first quarter. With English leading the way, there was a tangible trend toward excellence, rather than the senseless sinking into apathy that characterized many of the report cards I had seen that day. Mario grinned again, and then popped a question he had evidently been mulling.

"Whaddya give me if I make the honor roll?" he asked.

At Greenville High the honor roll is achieved merely by having a grade of B or above in all courses. I sometimes thought it should be called the "mediocrity roll," but nonetheless, fewer than 5 percent of the student body qualified. Because Mario took carpentry at the vocational center for two periods a day, he had only three grades in total. That meant he had to only pull two grades, in algebra II and carpentry, up to Bs in order to reach the honor roll. This was not an impossible feat by any means, but for Mario the aspiration was as foreign as running for student body president. Thrilled by the eagerness of his offer, I responded without thinking, trying to muster a challenge equally as audacious as the one that he proposed.

"I'll take you to lunch anywhere in Greenville you want to go!" I said. "You pick the place, I'll take you there and pick up the tab, as much as you can eat, I pay for!"

He smiled widely and extended his hand as he began to lean out the door, no doubt afraid to be seen talking to a teacher. I reached out and shook it, finalizing the agreement.

For Mario, the rest of the semester continued in a slow but perceptible ascent. He ended the semester with a 94 in my class, a very high B by Greenville's grading system, in which 95 or above was an A. His writing continued to improve, but he still lacked the fundamental study habits to prepare for exams and the discipline to keep abreast of daily homework—both of which he needed to earn an A. The semester ended and I bid Mario farewell for the Christmas holidays, making him promise that he would come find me when report cards were issued in January so that we could settle our bet.

By the time students received their report cards, it was almost the end of January. I was submerged in my three new courses and had all but forgotten about my bet with Mario when I saw him cresting the stairs with an uncontrollable grin. He handed his report card to me and shifted his feet as I opened it, trying to hide his pleasure. There was the B in English (94), a B in algebra II (87), and a C in carpentry that was crossed out with an 87 written next to it, initialed by the carpentry teacher. Mario quickly explained the carpentry grade. "I had some makeup work to do in carpentry," he said, "and I did it but he forgot to change the grade in the computer. But I went to him and he signed it."

"You did it!" I said. "You damn sure did it! You just tell me where we're going to lunch!"

I slapped him on the shoulder a half-dozen times and rubbed his head with a playful tug. I asked him repeatedly where we were going to eat and when, but it did not seem that important to him—the victory itself was still enough. He held the report card up and waved it, chuckling as he disappeared down the stairs.

I badgered him about planning his prize, but after a few reminders he seemed to be making little progress. Finally he asked if I would bring him some doughnuts instead. (One day I had brought in doughnuts to his class as a prize for an academic game; Mario had been on the team that won, and had cherished his doughnuts enough to make them last a couple of days—long beyond their own freshness.) I had been looking forward to a sit-down visit with Mario, but I was glad that he was going to cash in his reward in some form. I agreed to bring him a half-dozen doughnuts that Friday.

It was only Tuesday, and Mario must have reminded me ten times in the next two days to remember to bring his doughnuts. Friday morning, as my absentmindedness would have it, I did forget, and Mario came to me before the tardy bell to see if I had his prize. Covering my disappointment, I told him that I was going right after the bell, as first block was my conference period. Thankful for the reminder, after the bell rang I locked up my room and started for Shipley's Doughnuts. Two steps out the door I ran into Gus, a friend of Mario's, an equally shiftless and charming character who was not bothered by the fact that he was alone in the hallway and obviously tardy to class.

"You ain't really bringing Mario doughnuts today, are you? He's been going around all week telling folks you be bringing him doughnuts on Friday." He asked this with a wide smile, certain to get a denial from me which he could take back to deflate Mario's bragging.

"I sure am. I'm going to get them right now, and if you get to Spanish class, where you belong, you'll be there when I return to deliver them."

I returned with the doughnuts twenty minutes later, and after receiving approval from Mario's teacher, delivered them to his desk. It turned all the heads of his classmates. Mario sank deeper into his seat and smiled bigger, trying hard to hold in that chuckle he had let escape earlier. I saw Mario at lunch that day. He was still carrying his doughnuts, which were apparently untouched, and he was gathering a crowd. I watched him for most of the lunch period. This was his victory, and he would cherish it as long as possible.

At the end of each semester an awards ceremony was held in the auditorium, in which students who received A's or made the honor roll were recognized. The ceremony was long and tedious, but Mario was not mentioned, and his name was not on the honor roll list. Indignant at his omission, I searched for him after the ceremony, anxious to take our complaint to the counselor and make sure Mario received his certificate. I finally found Mario that afternoon leaning against the wall with some of his friends. He smiled at my agitation. Although Mario had been careful to ensure that the carpentry teacher had made the correction on his report card before he brought it to me, Mario was less adamant about making sure that the instructor changed the grade in the computer, and the teacher never did. As a result, that C was still in the computer.

Now even angrier, I prodded Mario to come to the counselor's office with me. For a moment he smiled unabashedly, "Ah, Mr. J., it don't matter. I already got my doughnuts."

Some weeks passed when I did not see Mario very often. I had begun coaching track and directing the senior play, and Mario's class schedule did not seem to bring him in a regular route past my door. Periodically I saw him and Gus walking the halls during first period and I always played dogcatcher—with a few instructive and comedic words I'd return them to their rightful owner. One day Mario would not look me in the face, but he giggled to himself, covering his mouth as I returned him to the room. When he glanced quickly up to say good-bye, I caught a glimpse of his badly bloodshot eyes, wandering in their glassy pools. I had thought that I smelled marijuana on him one morning earlier, but was reluctant to make an accusation. I drifted back to my room unsettled. A week later I was still without a plan when I ran into Mario during first block again. It was well after the bell and I was heading down to the office to turn in some paperwork.

At the time, Greenville High had a tardy policy whereby any tardy student had to report to one of the trailers behind the school to obtain a tardy slip before entering class. On most days the line extended a hundred yards down the walkway in the back of the building, but on rainy days it often turned inside and curled around the main staircase. I was halfway down the stairs when I spotted Mario and a friend of his hovering aimlessly at the end of the line. I reached Mario before he had a chance to spot me, and when I put a hand on his shoulder he turned, wincing. Upon recognizing me, he and his friend let out small laughs which they tried to control. Mario's eyes were fire red, and he seemed to be drowning behind them, lost beneath a hazy layer. He began to shrink away from me, still suppressing a giggle and averting his eyes as he saw me searching them. He stumbled back a few feet and bumped into the wall. This led his friend into uncontrollable giggles, and Mario couldn't help but emit a few himself. I was furious that I had not done something the first time.

Without thinking, I grabbed Mario by the arm and pulled him around the corner toward the teachers' lounge. I did not know Mario's friend, and what I had to say to Mario had nothing to do with him. Both of them were high on school property, but that was not the transgression I wanted to address. Mario and I had committed ourselves to an unspoken contract and this was a clear violation of it.

We rounded the corner and as I set Mario against the wall, his affect had already changed. No traces remained of the giggles or the smile, and his eyes fixed on the floor, evading the chastisement he knew was coming.

"What the hell are you doing coming to school high?" I said. "If you think I'm going to stand here and watch you burn that brain up, you're stone-cold crazy. I don't know who you're running with, but I'm going to find out, and when I do it's gonna stop. 'Cause whatever idiot passed you a joint at seven-thirty in the morning did it 'cause he doesn't have sense enough to do anything better. But you, you got the sense to do a hell of a lot better than this! What do you think all those comments on the back of your papers meant? Did you think I was making that up?

"When you had those doughnuts you had something. You know why? 'Cause you knew that you could do things people never dreamed you were capable of doing. And you liked that feeling. You liked that feeling of being known for something that mattered. Right now, you know what you're doing? You're telling everybody, 'You people were right, Mario ain't nothing. He's got no sense, no brains, and no desire to get them. He just wants to burn himself up until he's a useless old man propped on somebody else's porch drinking somebody else's booze.'

"Maybe Mr. Hudson isn't going to catch you. Maybe your sister and your mom aren't going to catch on for a while, either. But you know what, you're not getting away with it with me. You got too much up here to waste," I said, pointing to the side of his forehead, "and if you waste it, I haven't done my part, and you haven't done yours. Well, I'm going to make sure I do my part, and my part is to hold you to the standards that I know you can reach, so you better start reaching 'em. I don't ever, ever want to see this happen again. Now get to class, and start acting like the student you are instead of the thug these fools want you to be."

I turned and walked away. It wasn't until I got back to my room that I felt bad about how harsh my words had probably sounded. I had never felt more like a father, wanting to strengthen my child like tempered steel, but afraid to burn him in the fire.

A couple of days passed and I did not see Mario. I checked for him in the halls but he never appeared. I grew nervous about how to manage our next encounter. It was during my conference period when he appeared soundlessly at my doorway. He stumbled through the first few words, allowing his eyes to pass over my face only en route from one side of the room to the other. But the sight of them was bright and reassuring, like the beacon of a lighthouse at the instant it hits you squarely. His eyes were clear and crisp, lively in a way that I had nearly forgotten. He smiled again, but this time the shy and unassuming smile informed me that he had little practice in serious conversations. He pointed to my computer and mumbled to ask if he could use it to do a little research on a project he was doing on Frederick Douglass. Some months back one student had discovered the encyclopedia resource on my Encarta© CD-ROM, and since then I had played host to a steady stream of students who wished to use it to conduct research on reports they had to write for history class.

I did my best to be friendly to Mario, knowing how difficult it was for him to come to my room when he knew I would be the only one there. I also knew that my berating would be helpful only if Mario believed that it was because I cared about him. I got him oriented on the computer and looked over his shoulder as he found the entry for Frederick Douglass. I told him that I had a number of other resources on Frederick Douglass if he wished to see them, and returned to my desk to continue my own work. I wanted to talk, but I knew it had to be on Mario's terms, as he was the one that sought me out.

A few minutes later Mario broke the silence.

"What's this *Autobiography of Frederick Douglass*? He wrote that about himself, right?"

"Yes, he did."

"You got that?"

"Yes, I do, actually."

I searched the shelf and found my copy quickly, handing it to Mario. I began to give him an overview of it, but decided that it would be better explored on his own. He seemed to agree as he opened the book and quickly settled on a page that appealed to him. For the next forty-five minutes I checked on him periodically, but his face never left the book. It was the first time I had ever seen a student truly lost in learning in my room. The relevance to his assignment of what he was reading had long since been forgotten, and now he was simply lost on the desultory path of learning.

The last time that I looked up he was staring across the room and out the open windows. The book was closed but still he held it in his hands. I put down my pencil and quietly turned to face him. When our eyes met he hung his head slightly. Frederick Douglass had given him whatever strength he needed to begin our conversation. His face was calm now, and although still smiling his embarrassed smile, it was weighted with a wisdom and a patience that I had not seen there before. He fidgeted a moment with the book in his hand, a few times beginning to look up at me and then turning away. Still looking at the floor he spoke, timid and honest in a way that made his little voice quake: "Mr. Johnston, is a carpenter a good profession?"

In my career as a teacher, there has never been a moment that so profoundly broke my heart and renewed my hope in the same instant. At first I could not respond. There was so much in his pithy phrase that I did not know where to begin. That in my heart I knew he could aspire higher, that I did not know that much about how to become a carpenter or what it paid, that it was perhaps a dying craft in a technological world, these things were for now irrelevant.

"Yes, Mario," I said, "I think that a carpenter is a very good trade, and I think any team of carpenters would be lucky to have you."

He raised his head in a triumphant smile, and for the long second before he knew it and turned away, a single tear dove recklessly down his cheek.

After he left, I did not move for a long time, but stared out my window at that secret place that Mario had found after reading the words of Frederick Douglass. I have told Mario's story a half-dozen times, and a half-dozen times I have not been able to hold back tears. I am still confounded by it. I suppose the story tells itself in a way that I will never be able to retell. But I should add that there have been few times in my life that I have felt more integral to the project of life on this planet, more a part of that mysterious human quest for meaning, than I did in that room with Mario that day. I think it is the power of these rare moments of meaning that draw so many teachers back each fall.

When the bell rang I did not stir. I did not rise to shuffle papers or hustle to maintain the façade of preparedness. There was a new simplicity to what I did, a door that had opened before me to worlds I had not imagined. From where I sat, if you watched carefully you could marvel at it, like the impossible birth of a cottonseed or the slow rise of a wooden house: the steady construction of a man, built brick by brick from the shadow of a boy.

Part Four

IN THE DEEP HEART'S CORE

FIFTEEN

A t the beginning of my second year at Greenville High School,
I spent two full days decorating my classroom. I covered all
the chipped paint and permanent graffiti with forest green and
black marble adhesive paper, filling any open wall space with posters,
student work, quotations, pictures of great writers, scholarship
opportunities, essay contests, even newspaper cutouts of my home-
town Denver Broncos. With a bookshelf, rug, and three chairs that
I salvaged from other teachers, I created a reading center on one
side of the room and stocked it full of books, magazines, college
catalogs, and ACT preparation materials.

I had given up on fighting to keep the room mine, and sought
instead to make it belong to my students. The results were breath-
taking. In my first year, I could not erase the profanity on the walls
faster than it was written. I could not clean all the desks before the
ones at the beginning of the row had again been defaced. I had
covered one table with adhesive paper, but I had to recover it three
times in three months because students ripped the paper off in every
idle moment. Books were routinely scribbled in, huge lines of profanity written across every page.

But before my second year, I used more than four full rolls
of paper to cover the decaying walls and desks, and by the end of

the year not a piece had frayed and I had never replaced a spot. I never cleaned graffiti off a wall and only once did I stop to clean a desk, when the student sitting there apologized for her unconscious doodling and volunteered to do it herself. Several times I watched as students worked diligently to erase old profanities from books that were not theirs.

Whereas the first year had been replete with ridicule, harassment, and jokes every time I ventured into the hallway, in my second year I couldn't make it out my doorway without walking into a hug, a handshake, a question about track practice or August Wilson, or a student just smiling and pointing me out to a friend, "That's *my* teacher right there!" Most important of all, during chess club, ACT tutoring, track and soccer practice, play rehearsal, regular class time, and the hours before and after school, I was able to have thousands of conversations with students, ranging from the humorous to the tragic, the personal to the political. Where skepticism once reigned, friendships now emerged.

When I walked by classroom windows, student's faces would light up for a moment as I sent them a smile or a wave, and so would mine when—in the middle of a lesson—I would see the grin of a former student as she poked her head into my doorway. I stopped sitting down during lunch, as there were simply too many students I wanted to check in on to waste time sitting in one place. What was once my nemesis became my favorite part of the day, because it gave me the chance to find out how Jennifer's baby boy was doing, how Garland did at the Quiz Bowl, how Nikkia's drama school auditions went, and when Erica's next tennis match was.

My days were longer and busier than in the first year, the piles of work still taller on my kitchen table, but now there was a satisfaction in tending to them, an eagerness in the start of my truck each morning, and a deep sense of pride when the screen door slammed shut each night. I had discovered that feeling of redeeming exhaustion that comes when you work so hard for something you believe in. I had learned to love my exhaustion because it was the best evidence of the good I had done that day.

At Greenville all coaches had their planning period during fourth block in order to protect the school from needing to hire substitutes when teams had to leave school early for away games. Initially, this was a welcome change in the spring semester from the first-block planning period because it had the effect of making the day feel shorter: I was finished teaching at 1:50. Nonetheless, there were several complications that made fourth block less than a free period. Greenville High requires twenty-eight credits for graduation. However, on the block system a student takes four credits per semester, or thrity-two credits over the course of four years. If a student does well, or even passes all classes with Ds, he or she has fulfilled all graduation requirements by December of the senior year.

Seniors deal with this quirk in the system in several different ways. Those who have very good grades and are well respected by faculty and administration can apply for early release. This privilege allows a senior to take only one or two courses and leave school each day when those class periods are over. These seniors typically take two classes each semester and leave school at 11:30 every day. Some seniors simply take additional electives, but Greenville High does not have many electives and those it does have are egregiously overcrowded because they are the primary dumping ground for students who can't be placed anywhere else. Some of these seniors end up taking courses twice, as there is often no other available option but to go back for another semester of home economics or art or driver's education.

The third group of seniors consists of those who do not have good enough grades or the solid administrative support to be granted early release, yet they are not interested or not able to gain access to the few electives that are offered. These seniors become nomads for the last two periods of the day, not enrolled in any class and not allowed to leave the building. Their objective is simply to stay out of sight until the bell rings. The gym is the best hideout for these stowaways during the first three blocks but it closes for fourth block, which explains why they began to show up in my room.

My fourth-block class, as I came to call it, had a few permanent members, a dozen regulars, and an untold number of cameo appearances. David Perry was one of the permanent members. David went to the vocational center in the afternoons but did not have a fourth-block obligation there. Nonetheless, every day he managed to procure a ride from the vocational center back to school to arrive in my room in time for fourth block.

David had spent his childhood shuffling between his parents in Detroit and his grandmother in Greenville. After his mother and father died several years earlier in a car accident, he returned to Greenville to live with his grandmother full-time. Unfortunately, Greenville High had a difficult time verifying David's transcript from his Detroit school, and as a result Greenville High accepted only some of his credits and he was forced to repeat a significant part of his tenth-grade curriculum. He was consequently ineligible for graduation until the following year but had already completed nearly all his required courses.

David had taken English II with me and done quite well. Early in our in-class reading of *Julius Caesar* he grew enchanted with the character of Marc Antony. Every time we assigned parts, David pleaded to read Marc Antony. The most memorable moment of the semester came during our last day of reading *Julius Caesar*. I broke the class into five groups; each group was asked to create a ten-minute performance that captured the essence of one of the play's five acts. Students could choose whether they wanted to modernize the play or leave it in its historic context. David's group decided to modernize the play, placing the characters in contemporary settings and scenarios. Because this group spent so much time discussing setting and plot, they didn't have enough time to write out a formal translation or memorize lines. As a result, students had to read from the original Shakespeare text and invent a modern translation as they acted it out. Although the difficulty of this task caused some unnatural delays in the flow of the story, it also provided a good deal of humor and an impressive amount of creative insight.

In the climax of the drama, David, portraying the victorious Marc Antony, looked over Brutus's fallen corpse. The original text of Antony's moving eulogy reads:

> "This was the noblest Roman of them all:/ All the con-spirators, save only he,/Did that they did in envy of great Caesar;/ He, only, in a general honest thought,/ And common good to all, made one of them. His life was gentle; and the elements/ So mixed in him , that nature might stand,/ And say to all the world, 'This was a man!'"

David perused the text, took a long pause, and turned to the audience; "Lotta gangstas get into the game for the wrong reasons, but not this one. After all the players I seen wasting brothers for no good reason, Bruto ain't never played it like that. I ain't even gonna lie, Bruto didn't roll wit' my set, but this here is my true nig."

The crowd spontaneously erupted, students jumped to their feet, and even I could not resist the urge to drop to my knees and throw both hands triumphantly in the air. After that, David came to my class each semester when we read *Julius Caesar*. Most of the time he followed along quietly, but when no one else volunteered, he always jumped at the opportunity to read Antony. Eventually David began coming to my classroom whenever he could, regard-less of what we were studying. When the next school year began and he discovered he did not have a third-block obligation, it seemed only logical to assume that he would spend it in my room. He started a trend whereby old students of mine would procure passes to my room so they could sit and read along with us, join a discussion, or just revisit a favorite story or poem. Sometimes these visitors ended up immersed in a stack of magazines or college catalogs instead of following the lesson, but even that was preferable to laying their heads down or watching the clock tick someplace else.

Henry Kennedy was the second permanent member of my fourth-block class. Henry had English III during fourth block, but he took it with Ms. James, a permanent substitute. Although Ms. James did not have discipline problems, and was equitable and amiable with her students, very little English was ever covered. More than a few afternoons were spent watching movies that had no apparent connection to the course, and those were the active days. Ms. James had no objection to granting Henry a pass to my room at the beginning of fourth block every day. I would check with her occasionally to make sure Henry was abreast of all course work, which she always verified he was.

In my second year I had also taken the position as head coach of the soccer team. Henry was the captain of that team. Although only one person on the team had ever played competitive soccer before, the boys and girls who played did so with such passion that a culture had grown around them and the fledgling sport that had come to Greenville High only several years before. Although soccer was a winter sport in Mississippi, the team was constantly pushing me to call spring and summer practices "to get the gang together." On days when there was no track practice, I would notify Henry and he would gather the team.

On one day, all but two of our sixteen players had made it to the informal practice. Once I had changed and taken the field, Henry had already divided the teams for a full-field scrimmage.

"Whose team am I on?" I asked.

"The other one." Henry piped up from across the field. "We wouldn't take you."

"All right, Henry," I said. "What do you say, the losing team does two sets of sprints at the end, just for old time's sake?"

"Deal," Henry concurred, "and they pick up the balls."

"And they get dropped off last on the one-way!" came a shout from the other side of the field.

This generated a healthy cry of approval. None of the students on the soccer team had cars and only one of them had a parent who was able to pick him up after practice. As a result, part of every day's ritual involved seven to ten players piling into my truck after practice to be dropped off at home. When I first arrived in Mississippi, I was reluctant to transport students in the back of my truck because of safety concerns; most coaches and teachers had also advised me never to transport students for legal reasons. My resolve to abide by those inclinations lasted through the end of our second practice, when I saw the entire soccer team meandering slowly toward the highway. For the second straight day they began what, for some, would amount to a three- or four-mile walk home, so I decided to intervene. I compromised by resolving to drive carefully and stick predominantly to back roads.

The trip resembled an old milk route, following circuitous streets through small but distant neighborhoods, with a drop-off at each corner. In midseason one of the players had dubbed it the "one-way," as it was the one way home after practice. On a busy day the one-way could take as long as forty-five minutes, so a good place in the drop-off order was highly desirable.

"You got yourself a deal," I said, "losers get last drop on the one-way. Here we go."

Henry lived in Carver Circle, home to Greenville's most notorious gang—the Carver Circle Posse—and considered the most dangerous of all of Greenville's public housing projects. On most days Henry was dropped off last because he lived the farthest away, a coincidence that contributed substantially to the development of our friendship. Much to Henry's satisfaction, that afternoon he would be dropped off first.

Kenji Davenport was the third and final permanent member of my fourth block. Kenji's mother had died two years before, and because he was estranged from his father, he lived with a group of nuns in a local church. He had grown up in Chicago with his mother, and for two years she decided to keep Kenji out of school. After she died and he returned to Greenville, school had been a constant game of catch-up. Kenji had taken my Greek mythology class, and despite proving to be irresponsible about homework and long-term assignments, his memory for the nuances of Greek mythology was astounding. On a final exam where students had to answer twenty-five out of thirty short-essay questions, Kenji answered all thirty without an error. More impressive than that, Kenji accepted the challenge from a classmate to return the following semester and take the new Greek mythology exam without any review. Kenji accepted the challenge and answered twenty-nine out of thirty correctly.

In his final semester Kenji took only two classes because the counselors could not find him any electives. He was struggling to pass English IV in order to graduate, so he asked to sit in on my third-block English II class and then stay for tutoring during fourth block. Sometimes we went over grammar lessons, but Kenji spent the preponderance of his time asking me questions about the books he was supposed to be reading, and I spent the majority of my time encouraging him to read them. I helped where I could, sometimes clarifying issues of language or plot, but mostly providing a quiet place for him to get his reading done. He had a 62 at midterm because he had turned in his semester project late and not received credit. He needed to earn a 78 in his last nine weeks if he was to pass the course and graduate in May. The momentous significance of Kenji's English IV grades inspired and terrified him, causing erratic performances on tests and quizzes. Yet there was a singularity of focus to his time at school, and when fourth block was not crowded with its occasional visitors, his profound desire to graduate provided a more than adequate incentive to keep him on task.

Tiffany, Toni, and Kahlilah, three former students who had taken me up on my offer to help students prepare for the ACT, were also regulars in my fourth block. They all took chorus during fourth block and routinely came to my room when they had finished their perfunctory daily assignment.

Occasional guests in my fourth block might include a student who had missed the afternoon bus to the vocational center or any number of refugees who had been liberated from a stagnant class by a teacher who granted them a pass to my room. After they arrived, students often read magazines, worked on homework, or investigated college catalogs. And many came to play chess.

After rumors circulated that I had kept Larry after school to teach him some bizarre form of checkers, students began approaching me to ask if I would teach them as well. I brought my chessboard back to school and, within days, found more students eager to learn than I could find time to teach. It took only a couple of days watching fourteen students crowded around one chessboard to realize I needed to make an investment to remedy the situation.

I bought ten new chessboards at a clearance sale at a discount store and kept them stacked on top of the bookshelf in the reading corner. The boards were originally intended for use before or after school or during fourth block. However, on the first morning I brought the new boards to school, a number of students asked if they could take a board to class with them. Not wanting to provide an unnecessary distraction to students and teachers alike, I declined. Thirty minutes into our first period, one of the students returned to my door.

"Mr. J., can we please borrow a chessboard?" he asked. "We ain't doing nothing in there, and Ms. Chips say it's okay."

Curious, I walked the student back to the class to confirm that he had told the truth. When I knocked on the door to his classroom the answer was obvious: Four kids sat in a circle playing cards at the front of the room, a dozen had laid their heads dejectedly on their desks, and the rest chatted or watched the clock, willing it to move faster. I asked the teacher if it would be all right if the students played chess. She said it would be fine. Before the end of the day I had made several such walks to classrooms in various parts of the building, each scene more or less the same, each teacher responding in kind: "Sure, we ain't doing nothing right now." The next morning all ten chessboards were checked out before the bell rang for first block.

I was disappointed that the chess club would have to meet Wednesday mornings at 7:30 because I had track and soccer practice every day after school. There were no early buses to school and few kids had cars so I worried the turnout would be sparse. Much to my surprise, the first Wednesday fifteen students were waiting at my door when I arrived at 7:25. More surprising still, when I returned to school the next day, there were more than twenty-five kids assembled.

"Folks, chess club meets on *Wednesdays,*" I announced.

Henry responded, "I know Mr. J., this ain't chess club, we just *playing chess.*"

By Friday the chess club had burgeoned to nearly forty members, and any day that I wasn't in my room by 7:30 there were bound to be disgruntled chess players waiting. Chess at Greenville High was nothing like traditional chess games. No perfectly sterile rows of desks with silent, brooding competitors. In my room boards were set up on desks, on the floor, on people's backpacks, on top of filing cabinets and bookshelves. Each game had a peanut gallery that advised and scoffed at each move; each competitor delivered accompanied each move with a stream of commentary: "What? Buddy didn't see that coming, did he? Just plumb forgot about that knight, didn't you? See that's what happen when you get to worrying about that queen too much—Splackow!! The knight does you in! That's a'right, you just a rookie. Somebody come help this poor man out, he's bout to get torn up!"

Because fourth block tended to contain a high concentration of electives, the academic demands of these classes tended to fall far below the Greenville average. This meant that an exceedingly large number of students—especially chess club members—could easily obtain passes to come to my room because they "wasn't doing nothing" in their class. In addition to books, research, or tutoring, students could be sure to find a chessboard and a willing opponent in Mr. Johnston's fourth block.

Within a couple of weeks the chess team had burgeoned to almost forty members, claiming nearly as many students as the struggling Greenville High School football team. Together with my friend Wes Donehower, a fellow English teacher from the other public high school in town, we organized the first Greenville Chess Tournament in recent memory, inviting both the public schools and the white academies. For weeks leading up to the tournament, competition was vicious to determine our seeding. Some of the other schools could only field eight players so we had to maintain a ladder in my room that ranked all forty players. Only the top eight seeds would be allowed to compete in the tournament. The night before the tournament, numbers one through ten battled until dark, when those stuck at number nine and ten finally conceded to come along as alternates.

At 3:30 the following afternoon the team piled into my truck to head across town. We swept every team at the tournament. Two hours later we piled back into the truck in a disorderly cacophony, the truck bed shook as everyone shouted over each other to recount their highlights. We sat in the parking lot and laughed until the darkness came and everyone had told and retold the moment of their checkmate. We argued until we agreed on the moment when triumph caught like a grass fire and engulfed the room, teammates first gradually, and then contagiously started calling out "checkmate" to the nearest judge. The next day we were on the cover of the town paper, and chess players walked the halls like homecoming kings, earning the calm adoration of faculty, the flirtatious attention of the girls, the begrudging respect of the athletes. We organized several more tournaments after that one, and we never lost.

It was a Thursday and Kenji had settled into typing a paper for English class while Henry and David embarked on a game of chess and I began grading essays. We had passed ten minutes in silence when Tiffany pushed the door open. She was early for ACT tutoring and she was alone. I began to greet her when I noticed that she was fighting back tears.

She entered quietly, staring intensely at the ground, using that focus point to keep her composure the way one does on a balance beam. As she drew closer to me, her steps grew quicker, seemingly afraid that if she did not hurry she might break down before she reached my desk. Startled and frightened, I stood up. As I reached out to stablize her, she collapsed entirely, her legs buckling and her barely audible sniffle erupting into a plaintive sob. I caught her in my arms and strained to hold her on her feet as she cried effusively against my chest. Kenji, Henry, and David froze. I held her for a long moment as I waited for her to explain what had happened. Instead her sobs grew louder, her tears thicker, and her mouth shook uncontrollably each time she tried to speak.

"Tiffany, let's start at the beginning. Is everyone in your family okay?"

She nodded.

"Is it you, are you okay?"

She nodded again.

"That's a good start, is it a friend or a boyfriend that's in trouble?"

She nodded fervently when I said boyfriend.

"A boyfriend, is it Quin, is Quin okay?"

She began to cry still harder, but between sobs forced out two words.

"He's . . . shot."

"Okay, what do you say we walk a little?" She nodded again and with one arm still around her I guided her steadily toward the door.

"Kenji, you're in charge in here," I said before we left.

We walked the school grounds twice while she regained her composure, and settled in a remote stairway where I gradually ascertained the sequence of events. Tiffany's boyfriend worked at the local TV station with her. He had stayed home from school that day but awakened to the sound of breaking glass. When he stepped outside he found two men breaking into his sister's car and instinctively started down the driveway to chase them off. Spotting him, one of the men pulled a gun and shot Quin twice before they fled the scene without the car. Tiffany's chorus teacher also held down a part-time job at the TV station. He had been paged in the middle of the day when the station found out there had been a shooting that involved one of their young employees. He told Tiffany about it as soon as she arrived to chorus.

After a lengthy talk we went to the secretary's office to call the hospital to find out about Quin's situation and to call Tiffany's mother to pick her up. Because the hospital would not release information about patients over the phone, I left Tiffany with the secretary and drove over there to find that Quin was in stable condition. He had been shot through the cheek and the shoulder without any major damage, predominantly superficial wounds that would heal soon. I made it back to school just as the bell rang—in time to give

Tiffany the good news and walk her to her mother's car. I gave Tiffany my phone number in case she needed anything and told her I would call to check up on her before the day was over.

The school had emptied and the buses had departed by the time I made it back to my classroom. The door to my room was open and I was surprised to see Kenji, David, and Henry still sitting quietly inside. Kenji broke the silence. "Everything all right?"

I usually spent fourth block grading papers, tutoring a student, occasionally playing chess, or indulging in a conversation with Kenji, Henry, and David, but I often made excursions to converse with Mr. Ransom, a chemistry teacher. Mr. Ransom was part of the cabinet of outstanding teachers on whom I leaned heavily for support and guidance. Ms. Striebeck, who taught math, and Ms. Lewis, who taught social studies, were constant resources for pedagogy and curriculum; Coach Ward (also a chemistry teacher, former basketball coach, and constant father figure) and my good friend Coach Pierson for discipline; Ms. Winford and Ms. Fowles—both social studies teachers—for student and family relations; my neighbors, Ms. Williams and Ms. Pittman, for English questions; Mr. Woodard and Ms. Gladys Smith for leadership in student activities; and Mr. Ransom for points of philosophical or historical inquiry.

Mr. Ransom had been raised in the Mississippi Delta, had attended one of its historically black colleges, and was working on his Ph.D. in advanced chemistry from Jackson State. He had first caught my attention when I overheard him say that he had spent the last couple of years teaching in Mound Bayou, Mississippi. Mound Bayou is considered the oldest black municipality in the country, founded by slaves fleeing Delta plantations after the end of the Civil War. Though he had enjoyed a comfortable teaching job at his old school in Greenwood, Ransom had moved to Mound Bayou because he believed it was "a part of Mississippi every black man should know."

Mr. Ransom was one of the teachers who captured student interest by staying deeply connected to the world the students inhabited. He knew all the hottest rap and R & B bands, the en vogue movies and phrases; in fact, he helped launch several of the Delta's most successful rap groups when the boys were students of his. He was also a Muslim, which set him apart in a significant way from the almost uniformly Baptist black community in Greenville. Our friendship was built on the fact that he found a peculiar joy in contemplating the problems of the universe.

Frequently, in the middle of the day, one of Mr. Ransom's students would arrive at my door with a note containing something like the following: "Mr. J., if the only way to the Christian heaven is through works *and* faith, is Gandhi burning in hell? Would love to hear your thoughts." Or, "Mr. Johnston, if the goal of science is to resolve the mysteries that remain in the world, why do we teach science to children? Wouldn't we be better off teaching them the mysteries instead of the answers?"

On days such as those I would spend the first five minutes of fourth block composing a response. If his class was busy when I arrived at his door, I would knock and quietly hand him my response with a smile.

"Thank you, Mr. Johnston," he would say. "This will give me something to ponder for the evening."

On other days, Mr. Ransom would see me through the door and prepare a grand entrance. "Mr. Johnston, a pleasure to have you here to share some wisdom."

As the class grew to appreciate our intellectual interludes, Mr. Ransom would often ask me to present my opinions before the class. On days like these he would probe the students for their own reactions before offering his own response, thanking me, and returning to the subject of chemistry.

* * *

May was a nervous month for my fourth block. Kenji took his English IV final exam the first week of May, but would not know his final grade until the counselors called him in to verify his transcript and issue him a cap and gown if he had successfully qualified. Because this occurred only three days before graduation, this was a tremendously emotional moment. As parents and seniors congested the hallway around the counselor's office, nearly every meeting yielded elation or despair, relief or hysteria. Students whose families had already traveled across the country for the ceremony were told they weren't going to graduate; freshman-year missteps and careless class selection punctured the visions of more than a few expectant seniors. Kenji had to go to the counselor's alone on that important day because he did not have a formal guardian.

Kenji continued coming to school even after he had taken his final exam and seniors were through with classes. On these days he stayed in my room from 8:00 in the morning until 3:45 in the afternoon. Rarely did an hour pass that Kenji didn't bring up the test, replaying the questions he might have missed, recalculating the averages of his existing grades, speculating on what he would do if he couldn't graduate.

The last week of the year was unusually quiet in the fourth block. With the seniors gone and all other classes preparing for final exams, the number of students obtaining passes to my room had slowed to a trickle. Most days it was only Kenji, David, Tiffany, Henry, and I. When the fateful moment arrived for Kenji to go to the counselor for his grades, we each gave him a hug and sent him on his way, and then we waited. We neither spoke nor worked, but mostly feigned preoccupation to pass the time. Tiffany pulled a disposable camera out of her purse and began unwrapping it. As I watched her, she noticed me and smiled self-consciously. "I didn't want to make him nervous, you know . . . in case it don't work out."

"Oh, it's gonna work out," David interjected. "Don't you worry about that. My boy's on it this time."

In the Deep Heart's Core

Stories of students denied and students approved permeated the hallways: one mother hollering at the principal when her son was denied a diploma, one mother crying right on the counselor's shoulder when she got the good news. Fifteen minutes later, I was still grading the same vocabulary quiz when the door swung open. Both of Kenji's fists were thrust in the air just high enough that the edges of his shirtsleeves protruded from the ends of the black gown, his cap perched squarely on his head. He looked a foot taller and his lean frame fifty pounds heavier. Tiffany screamed and David pumped one fist into the air. Kenji's transformation was more than symbolic. The long black gown bestowed an unshakable dignity on a boy who a moment earlier was nervous, restless, painfully conscious of the awkwardness in his every movement.

After I got dressed for graduation, I returned to school to help haul graduation materials to the convention center. I too had bought a camera for the occasion and it perched proudly on the front seat of my truck. I loaded the last box and glanced at my watch: The seniors would be arriving now. From all the quiet, lonely sections of Greenville, a massive march had gathered its faithful and now pushed toward the convention center with a modest but insistent dignity. Sketched in dusk, Greenville High looked on with a parent's humility, urging me to go and join the others. The Mississippi spring gathered in the warmth of the darkness with neither a memory of the cold winter nor a harbinger of an oppressive summer. Her seasons already felt familiar, the air suffused with a delicate heat that caressed with every step. My truck's ignition coughed and caught and soon the dim lights of Greenville High retreated into darkness.

SIXTEEN

The first time I taught a unit on poetry, one of my classes was having difficulty understanding rhyme and meter. On one long afternoon, we had already reviewed all the poems in our literature book but the students were still confused. Short of material, I pulled out a stack of old literature books that we had never used, hoping they might provide some new poems. Most of the books were without spines and many without covers, but those that didn't have the pages torn out contained a sizable selection of poetry. Anxious to practice scansion with some unfamiliar poems, I turned to the first poem in the book, W. B. Yeats's "The Lake Isle of Innisfree":

> I will arise and go now, and go to Innisfree,
> And a small cabin build there, of clay and wattles made:
> Nine bean-rows will I have there, a hive for the honey-bee,
> And live alone in the bee-loud glade.
>
> And I shall have some peace there, for peace comes dropping
>   slow,
> Dropping from the veils of the morning to where the cricket
>   sings
> There midnight's all a glimmer, and noon a purple glow,
> And evening full of the linnet's wings.

I will arise and go now, for always night and day
I hear lake water lapping with low sounds by the shore;
While I stand on the roadway, or on the pavements grey,
I hear it in the deep heart's core.

It was the last line that first caught my attention. I had once heard a Mississippian tell me, "If Mississippi is the heart of the Deep South, then the Mississippi Delta is the deep heart's core." That was, after all, the reason I came.

The history of slavery, Jim Crow and segregation, the extreme poverty, the enduring chasms of race and class: All of these ills bear down on the Delta like the heat of the sun focused through a magnifying glass, threatening at any moment to set the landscape with flames. The ghosts of our great civic soldiers and their dreams of social justice linger strongest here, their restless souls not yet convinced that their work has been completed. You can feel them hovering over the graveyards and the schoolyards, the courthouses and the jailhouses, letting the weight of their watching compel us to right ourselves and steer toward a new horizon.

But what Yeats spoke of was an entirely different deep heart's core, a place of solitude and peace where a beleaguered man could seek solace from the chaos and distraction of his life. Where, I began to wonder, was that retreat for my students? For those who made their lives here in the core of the Old South, what world did they envision as an escape? What ideal did they dream of inside their own hearts' deep core?

These questions moved me enough that I decided to change my teaching plan for the day. After quickly closing our discussion of rhyme and meter, I asked students to imagine in their journals a peaceful haven of their own like the one Yeats dreamed of in his poem: I asked them to construct their very own Innisfree. A handful chose ten Mercedes-Benzes, million-dollar houses in Beverly Hills, and a harem of movie-star lovers. But the preponderance expressed no such wish. They envisioned something different, something sane and simple.

People who spend the majority of their lives in transit and in a hurry, in a time of revolution and tumult, as Yeats did, long for a place like Innisfree, where the water is quiet and the sky is wide. It is one of life's ironies that those who have much yearn to be returned to the state of having little. The opposite is often believed to be true of those who have very little—that they long to have everything. But that appears to be far from true. Those who can only afford to keep a few dollars' worth of gas in their car still find a few spare moments to dream of the world that might be, of an isle like Innisfree. Even students who live ten miles from a grocery store, who have never traveled farther than the county line, possess an image of a very simple paradise. Reading those journal entries the following night moved me to write this book.

In making the Delta my home, I found inside her a despair beyond any I could have imagined, often surpassing the tragedies of Delta generations past. But in the end this always moved me less than the overwhelming power of hope that throbbed beneath and beyond destitution's long, heavy breaths. When I read those essays, I was at first disappointed by the simplicity of my students' visions. I worried that perhaps they aspired to mediocrity. It was only after reading the seventh or eighth entry that I came to understand that dreams consist of filling in the absences we perceive in our own world. Each of the essays had done just that.

Kristol described her Innisfree this way: "At the end everybody would get what they rightfully deserve. All the girls would graduate and make something out of themselves and so will the boys. When they get older they will have their own jobs in law firms and clothing stores and restaurants. They will be able to enjoy their young years before they have to worry about having children. Once they make that decision they will have jobs and be married, have two or three kids. They each have big enough houses for their family and they don't have to worry about living off their spouse or paying the bills. That is my Innisfree."

The beauty and the pathos in Yeats's poem come not from his description of Innisfree, but from the tension established between the "greyness" of the present and the "glimmer" of the future. In a dismal moment he retreats into his deep heart's core to find solace in the promise of a better world. In the heart of the Old South, generations upon generations have passed in which a black childhood can wither and die without ever finding its way to a place where "peace comes dropping slow." So we are tempted to believe them dead before they are born, expired before they have begun.

But like Yeats, in their deep hearts' core these children harbor visions of a world that glimmers, snapshots of an existence that offers meaning and dignity. For Yeats, that vision was an actual memory of a real place, a place to which he longed to return. In Greenville it is more complicated. Although a young girl may craft an Innisfree inside her heart, she cannot leave the bustle of her ordinary world and travel to that place, as Yeats did, because she is not sure that it exists. She must try to transform her own world to match that vision if she is ever to live there.

Though much has changed in the generation since the freedom riders rode into Mississippi and the Poor People's March walked out, the Innisfree that my students describe is to them still a myth—a world where they can all live decently and happily without the daily fear of dying or the crushing pressure of paying the bills. What is astonishing is that there is still hope that they will reach that place. Here in the very core of the Deep South, even after atrocity and indignity, the human spirit shakes and stirs and threatens to rise up again. Still, hope endures, for one can feel it rising here, in the deep heart's core.

Endnote

At Greenville High School, I was first and foremost a teacher. This meant I had the opportunity to know the students, staff, and families in this book with a complexity unattainable for a journalist or a researcher. But I never carried a tape recorder or took formal notes during conversations, and so the dialogue in this book is carefully reconstructed from my own memory.

The names of students included in this book have been changed in instances when I thought it inappropriate to expose such information about a child, when the appearance was brief enough to be insubstantial, or when I could not locate the student to review his or her section of the book.

In all other instances, I allowed students to read their sections of the book and decide whether I should use their own names or a fictional name of their choosing. Henry, Marvin, David, Kenji, Corelle, Chico, Tiffany, Dianca, Derrick, and Melinda want you to know that their names are accurate, and I want you to know that this book does not begin to capture their deep goodness, for which I am forever grateful.

With adults, I stuck to the simple mantra that if I did not have nice things to say, I did not use the person's real name. I believe anyone who has lived in and loved a small town will understand that choice. On a deeper level the purpose of this book was not to expose any individual for ridicule or responsibility, but to provide one perspective on poverty, race, and education in the Delta. Individual naming and shaming adds nothing to that project. Mr. McCormick's name is real and if you're ever looking for a good conversation about the Delta I urge you to stop by McCormick's Book Inn when you're in Greenville.

Early on I decided to make this a book about students, although an equally interesting and moving account might have been rendered of the teachers who comprise Greenville High School. As a result of that choice, my fellow teachers and other Delta friends are absent from this book in a way that misrepresents the profound impact they had on my personal life, my work, and my love for Mississippi. A brief mention of some of them in the final section is my paltry attempt to thank them for the incredible support and friendship they provided.

Over the course of several years the moments that stand out in any recollection are the unusual ones—either for their tragedy or triumph. This should not obscure the fact that Greenville High School is a high school like many others, where hundreds of students and teachers come to school every day to work hard at the tasks before them. If I have learned anything since leaving Greenville, it is that the struggles young people face there persist in classrooms and communities all over this country. Students in Chicago and Colorado and Connecticut confront inequality and grapple with poverty every day. Though Mississippi has so often been in the spotlight because of civil unrest, it has also spent decades directly confronting the difficult issues of race and class that many other parts of America continue to avoid. This book shows these universal challenges as they exist in Mississippi only because I had the good fortune to live there.

Greenville High School has seen drastic improvements in its facilities, faculty, and spirit since I began writing this book under the leadership of a new superintendent, Dr. Arthur Cartlidge. My former colleague Leeson Taylor, an inspiring and charismatic history teacher and GHS alum, is now the new principal. I am proud to say that as I write this, Greenville is waging a noble war for educational improvement, and succeeding far better than most.

When I arrived in the Delta I knew that I might not stay forever, but hoped that my experiences there would teach me lessons I could carry on to other communities in other states. I could not have anticipated that I would grow to love the Delta with the ferocity of a native son. I now consider Mississippi my second home, and hope that Mississippians will understand this book is meant as an expression of profound gratitude; if that is unclear it is a failure of my skill rather than my sentiment.

Acknowledgments

I am deeply grateful to the brain trust that convinced me this book was possible and nurtured it through a long infancy: Cynthia Farrar, Doug Rae, Tamar Gendler, Gary Orfield, Robert Coles, and my agent, Sterling Lord. I extend my sincerest thanks to Tom White for his invaluable work on the early drafts and to Andy Callahan for his intuition. To Brendan Cahill, my editor at Grove/ Atlantic, this book was truly blessed to have fallen into your hands, and so was I.

To my own legion of outstanding teachers, especially Mr. Abuisi, Mr. Bandoni, and Mr. Schindel, I am so thankful for how much of you I continue to find in myself.

Special thanks to Johnny, not only for the ways his wisdom has shaped this book, but for the ways his goodness has shaped my life.

And for Courtney, who lived every page of this book with me, who is the reason I love the south so deeply and the reason I'll never leave it behind.